CONTENTS

The following people made special contributions to this book:

Edmond Ho, my brother, photographer and my friend, who helped inspire me to embark on this project;

David Yip and the team at Marshall Cavendish International (Asia) Pte Ltd, who believed in this book and worked tirelessly and patiently throughout the project;

My supportive and loving family, Joanne Ho, Timothy Ho and Fiona Ho;

Frankie, Irene and Wong who helped me test recipes and develop most of the dessert recipes;

My parents, for their love and belief in my career choice;

Management team of SATS Catering Pte Ltd for its support;

Peter Knipp, a chef and mentor;

Patrick Ng, Managing Director of Potterhaus Singapore, for the stunning handmade glasswares;

Roger Hague Associates, Narumi Singapore Pte Ltd, Sia Huat Private Limited, Takashimaya Department Store Household Interiors Department and The Life Shop for the loan of their crockery and utensils.

The Publisher wishes to thank Roger Hague Associates, Narumi Singapore
Pte Ltd, Sia Huat Private Limited, Potterhaus Singapore, Takashimaya
Department Store Household Interiors Department and The Life Shop for
the loan of their crockery and utensils.

Chef : Anderson Ho
Project Editor : Jamilah Mohd Hassan
Art Direction/Designer : Christopher Wong
Photographer : Edmond Ho
Prop Stylists : Lydia Leong and Yeo Puay Khoon
Editor : Yeo Puay Khoon
Production Co-ordinator : Nor Sidah Haron

Published by Times Editions – Marshall Cavendish
An imprint of Marshall Cavendish International (Asia) Private Limited
A member of the Times Publishing Limited
Times Centre, 1 New Industrial Road, Singapore 536196
Tel: (65) 6213 9288 Fax: (65) 6285 4871
E-mail: te@tpl.com.sg
Online Bookstore: http://www.timesone.com.sg/te

Malaysian Office:
Federal Publications Sdn Berhad (General & Reference Publishing)
(3024-D)
Times Subang, Lot 46, Persiaran Teknologi Subang
Subang Hi-Tech Industrial Park, Batu Tiga, 40000 Shah Alam
Selangor Darul Ehsan, Malaysia
Tel: (603) 5635 2191 Fax: (603) 5635 2706
E-mail: cchong@tpg.com.my

National Library Board (Singapore) Cataloguing in Publication Data

Ho, Anderson, 1964-
Menu degustation : tasting menus of new Asia cuisine / Anderson Ho ;
photography by Edmond Ho. - Singapore : Times Editions, c2003.
p. cm.
ISBN : 981-232-655-3

1. Cookery, Asian. I. Ho, Edmond, 1967- II. Title.
TX724.5.A1
641.595 — dc21   SLS2003033687

Printed in Singapore by Fabulous Printers Pte Ltd

MENU
TASTING MENUS OF NEW ASIA CUISINE
DéGUSTATION

ANDERSON HO
PHOTOGRAPHY BY EDMOND HO

TIMES EDITIONS

MENU DéGUSTATION

TASTING MENUS OF NEW ASIA CUISINE

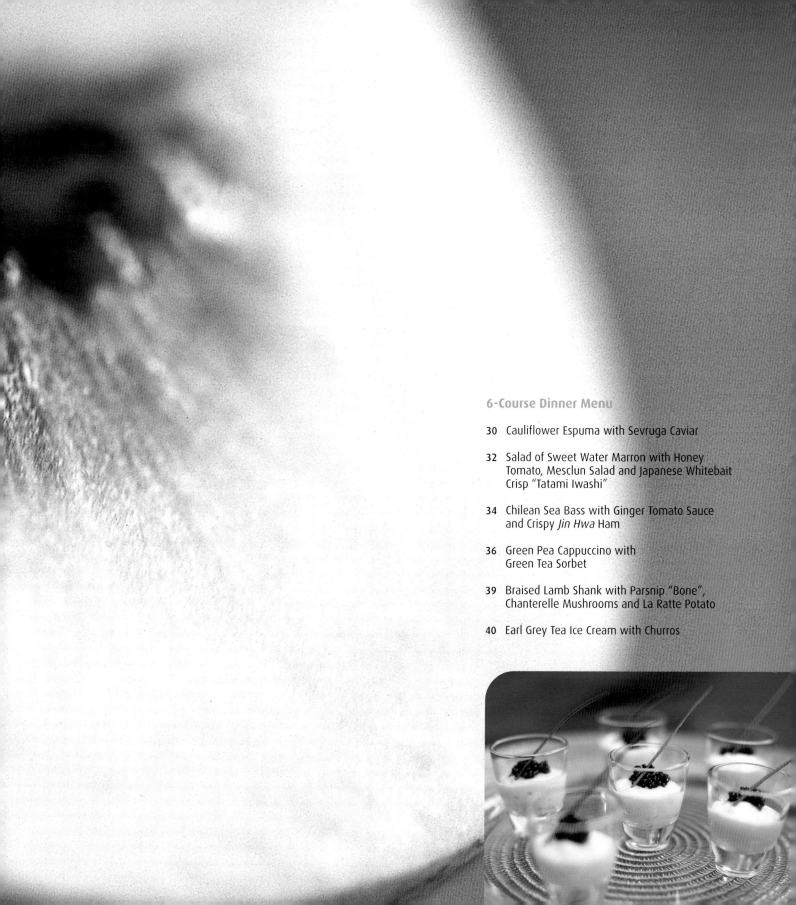

7-Course Dinner menu

CONTENTS

8-Course Dinner Menu

10-Course Dinner Menu

CONTENTS

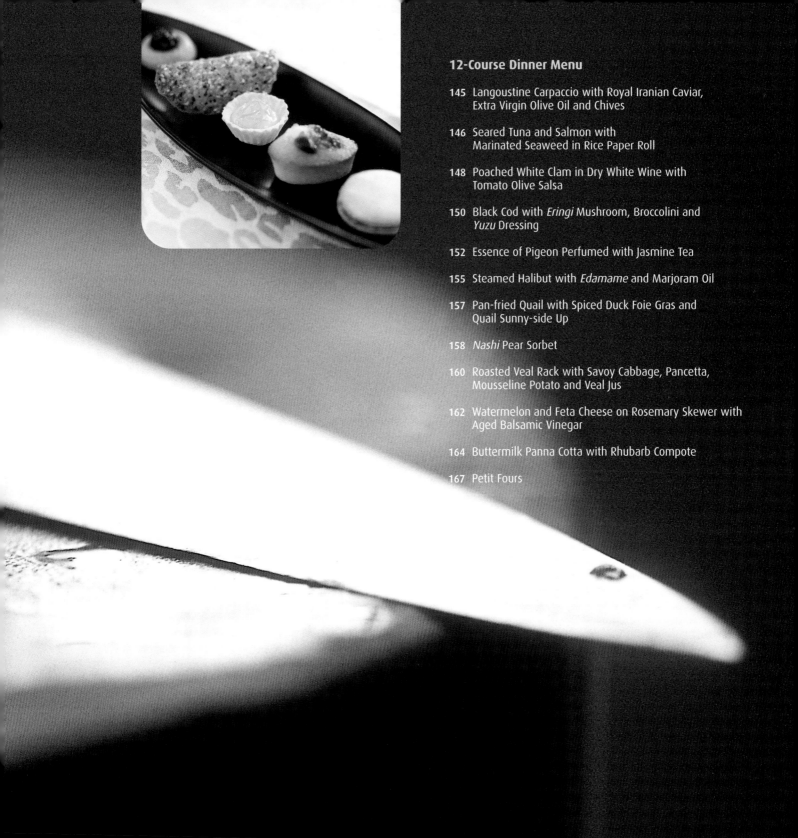

12-Course Dinner Menu

FOREWORD

HIS talent is unmistakable. The visual evidence in the pages of this book alone should convince you of that, but having tasted his creations on numerous occasions, it bears testimony that pictures in this book are only tickling one of the senses that stimulate gastronomic excitement. I have known Anderson for 12 years now, and every encounter has been a rewarding one. Watching him mature from a young chef into professional, all have come to appreciate the immense talent and dedication in this unassuming person. Throughout his career his quiet flair for food clings like a perfectly fitted cloak to his capable shoulders.

His secret is probably this: though today, he is already well established in his field, with years of travel, exposure, learning and competitions behind him, he still has the heart and imagination

of a young chef fascinated by life and new things. Coupled with an inventor's ambition, these qualities make Anderson an ideal candidate for pushing the boundaries of what can be accomplished in the Asian high-temple of gastronomy, Singapore.

New Asia Cuisine is incredibly hard to define and master, but with praiseworthy courage and focus, I think he has chosen a path many chefs aspire to, but few have had the desire to pursue. He now has in his hands the creation of a legacy, which he can leave for his disciples in the culinary profession, the aspiring young professionals that are constantly looking out for a master. I hope that you are able to look beyond the pretty pictures and methodology of each dish featured in this book, and see the reflection of one who is ready to dare, to pursue and to share – the qualities we are looking for when searching for role-models.

I am humbled that Anderson has asked me to write the foreword to his book. May his culinary zeal inspire many to reach greater culinary heights.

Peter A Knipp
Managing Director, Peter Knipp Holdings Pte Ltd
Co-organiser, World Gourmet Summit Singapore

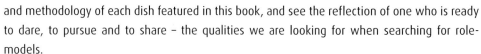
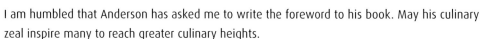

5 - COURSE

CRABMEAT ROLL
Smoked Salmon and Crabmeat Roll

INGREDIENTS

Salmon and Crabmeat Roll

Smoked salmon slices	4, 20 g each
Mud crabmeat	80 g, cooked
Spring onion (scallion)	3 g, finely chopped
Celery	12 g, brunoise
Green apple	20 g, brunoise
Yuzu zest	2 g
Mascarpone cheese	40 g
Salt and pepper	a pinch

Garnishing

Oba leaves	4
Crème fraîche	40 ml
Salmon roe	20 g
Shisho leaves	4

METHOD

Salmon and Crabmeat Roll

· Mix crabmeat with spring onion, celery, green apple, *yuzu* zest and Mascarpone cheese. Season to taste.

· Lay a salmon slice on a sheet of cling film. Place a second slice on top, overlapping the first slice lengthwise. Place a few spoonfuls of crabmeat mixture in the centre and roll up tightly lengthwise.

· Twist and tie both ends, making sure that both ends are tight. Refrigerate 5-6 hours before serving.

· Cut through cling film with sharp knife to portion.

Garnishing

· Serve roll on a piece of *Oba* leaf. Top with a dollop of crème fraîche and a generous helping of salmon roe. Garnish with *Shisho* leaf.

INGREDIENTS

Duck Confit

Duck legs	2
Thyme	1 g
Rosemary	1 g
Garlic	5 cloves
Shallots	5, peeled
Freshly cracked black peppercorn	a pinch
Coriander seeds	a pinch, grounded
Rock salt	a pinch
Duck fat	500 ml
Duck foie gras	30 g, diced
Salt and pepper	a pinch
White port wine	30 ml
Wanton wrappers, round	4
Fresh water chestnut	10 g, peeled and diced
Spring onion (scallion)	3 g, chopped
Winter truffle	5 g, brunoise

Port Wine Reduction

Port wine	100 ml
Cold butter	50 g, cubed
Duck jus	100 ml
	(see Basic Techniques pg 174)

Sautéed Foie Gras

Vanilla bean	1
Honey	100 ml
Kamquat	200 g, sliced
Red wine vinegar	30 ml
Water	40 ml
Duck foie gras slices	4, 40 g each
Plain (all-purpose) flour	for dusting
Freshly cracked black peppercorn	a pinch
Sea salt	a pinch

Foie Gras Crème Brulee

Duck foie gras	100 g
Egg	1
Egg yolk	1
Cream	250 g
Brandy	a dash
Salt and pepper	a pinch

Garnishing

Apple balsamic vinegar	10 ml
Green apple	1, cut into small wedges

METHOD

Duck Confit

- Marinate duck with thyme, rosemary, garlic, shallots, black pepper, coriander seeds, rock salt and duck fat overnight.

- Drain and reserve marinade. Sear duck leg over high heat until browned. Replace in marinade and cook in oven at 90°C for 2–2½ hours, until meat almost separates from bones.

- Debone and shred duck confit. Mix with duck foie gras. Season to taste. Add a dash of white port.

- Scoop 1 teaspoon of duck mixture onto wanton wrapper. Fold wrapper over filling into a semi-circle and seal edges with water.

- Line a bamboo steamer with a banana leaf, brushed with oil to prevent sticking. Steam dumplings over high heat for 3–5 minutes.

Port Wine Reduction

- Monte port wine in a saucepot with a few cubes of cold butter. Whisk vigorously as you add butter in stages. Reduce port wine by half. Season to taste.

Sautéed Foie Gras

- Split vanilla bean and scrape out vanilla seeds. Pour honey into a pot and add vanilla seeds. Caramelise until dark brown. Add sliced kumquat, red wine vinegar and water. Cook for 3–5 minutes.

- Dust foie gras lightly with flour. Shake off excess flour. Sauté on both sides until brown. The middle should still be soft. Serve with kumquat compote and sprinkle with freshly cracked black peppercorn and sea salt.

Foie Gras Crème Brulee

- Blend all the ingredients except brandy in a food processor until smooth. Add brandy. Season to taste. Pass through a fine sieve. Pour into a shot glass, filling up to the brim.

- Line gastronome tray with cloth then place the shot glass on cloth. Fill tray with hot water until three-quarter height of shot glass. Cover tightly with aluminium foil. Poach in an oven at 100°C for 1 hour.

- Sprinkle sugar on top of crème brulee and use a handheld torch to melt sugar until caramelised.

- Serve with a few drops of apple balsamic vinegar. Garnish with green apple wedges.

- Arrange dumpling, sautéed foie gras and foie gras crème brulee on a plate and serve.

DUCK FOIE GRAS

Variations of Duck Foie Gras

- Duck Confit and Foie Gras Dumpling with Port Wine Sauce
- Sautéed Foie Gras with Kamquat Compote
- Foie Gras Crème Brulee

ROASTED COD CHEEK
Cream of Celeriac with Roasted Cod Cheek and Tomato Fondue

YIELDS 1.5 LITRES

INGREDIENTS

Celeriac Soup
Canola oil	50 ml
White onion	80 g, peeled and chopped
Thyme	2 g
Smoked bacon	30 g
Celeriac	300 g, peeled and roughly cut
Leek, white part only	30 g
Chicken stock	1 litre
	(see Basic Techniques pg 174)
Cream	200 ml

Cod Cheek
Cod cheeks	4, 40 g each
Salt and pepper	a pinch
Olive oil	30 ml

Tomato Fondue
Fresh tomato	1 kg
Extra virgin olive oil	50 ml
Thyme	1 g, finely chopped
Red onion	100 g, peeled and finely chopped
Sugar and salt	a pinch

Garnishing
Chervil

METHOD

Celeriac Soup
- Sweat onions, thyme and smoked bacon. Add in celeriac later, followed by leek and chicken stock. Cook it down until celeriac is soft. Add cream. Cook for another 5 minutes. Remove smoked bacon and purée in blender then pass through a fine sieve. Season to taste. The consistency of the soup can be adjusted by adding more stock if it is too thick.

Cod Cheek
- Season cod cheek with salt and pepper. Heat olive oil and pan-fry until golden brown on both sides.

Tomato Fondue
- Purée fresh tomato, thyme and red onion in a blender and pass through a fine sieve. Add olive oil, sugar and salt, and cook it down to a paste over low heat.

- Serve soup in a soup bowl with cod cheek. Top with a tomato fondue quenelle and garnish with chervil.

INGREDIENTS

Herb-crusted Beef Tenderloin

Beef tenderloin	600 g, trimmed
Rosemary	2 g, freshly chopped
Thyme	2 g, freshly chopped
Olive oil	20 ml
Salt and pepper	a pinch
Chives	20 g, chopped
Flat parsley	20 g, chopped

Morel Mushroom Sauce

Dried Morel mushrooms	25 g, reconstituted, washed and trimmed
Butter	30 g
Olive oil	30 ml
Madeira wine	125 ml
Veal jus	100 ml (see Basic Techniques pg 174)
Balsamic vinegar	20 ml
Fingerling potato	100 g, sliced at 5-mm thickness
Salt and pepper	a pinch
Honey tomatoes	16
Pencil asparagus	80 g, peeled, trimmed and blanched
Edamame beans	60 g, blanched and peeled

METHOD

Herb-crusted Beef Tenderloin

· Tie beef tenderloin firmly with butcher's meat string at 2-cm intervals. This will help the beef tenderloin retain its shape even after cooking while preventing excessive shrinkage. Marinate beef with rosemary, thyme, olive oil, salt and pepper for half an hour. Sear beef tenderloin on all sides in a heavy cast-iron sauté pan and roast at 120°C for about 20–30 minutes until just pink in the middle. Transfer beef to a tray and remove the butcher's string. Spread chopped chives and parsley all over beef tenderloin and rest for 15 minutes before portioning.

Morel Mushroom Sauce

· Sweat the Morel mushrooms in a pan at medium high heat with a dollop of butter and olive oil. Deglaze pan with Madeira wine and reduce by a third. Add veal jus and balsamic vinegar; reduce further until a rich syrupy consistency is achieved. Pass sauce through a fine sieve and whisk in a few cubes of cold butter. Keep Morel mushrooms aside until ready to use.

· Roast sliced potato in a preheated oven at 200°C for 10–15 minutes until golden brown and cooked. Season potatoes with salt and pepper.

· Sauté tomatoes, asparagus and *edamame* in olive oil and season with salt and pepper.

· Cut beef into 4 portions of approximately 120 g each. Serve with sautéed vegetables, Morel mushrooms and Morel mushroom sauce.

BEEF TENDERLOIN
Herb-crusted Beef Tenderloin with Morel Mushroom Sauce

INGREDIENTS

Bread and Butter Pudding

Vanilla bean	1
Milk	125 ml
Cream	125 ml
Castor sugar	35 g
Eggs	2, large
Day-old white bread or butter croissants, sliced	4 slices
Butter	for spreading
Castor sugar	for sprinkling
Dehydrated berries	15 g

Whisky Ice Cream

Egg yolk	320 g
Granulated sugar	200 g
Trimoline	200 g
Milk	1 litre
Vanilla bean	1
Cream	500 g
Whisky	120 ml

Tuile

Butter	50 g
Confectioner's sugar	50 g
Egg white	50 g
Plain (all-purpose) flour	50 g

Berry Compote

Dehydrated berries	100 g
Castor sugar	50 g
Water	100 ml

METHOD

Bread and Butter Pudding

· Split vanilla bean and scrape out seeds. Mix milk, cream, sugar and egg together. Add in vanilla seeds and mix well. Spread each slice of bread with butter. Butter a loaf tin and sprinkle with castor sugar. Arrange slices by overlapping each slice over another. Sprinkle dehydrated berries while overlapping slices. Repeat until the tin is filled up to the top.

· Strain cream mixture and pour over bread until all the bread is soaked. Let it stand for at least 30 minutes. Bake at 170°C for 30–40 minutes, depending on the height of the tin, until golden brown.

Whisky Ice Cream

· Mix egg yolk and sugar together and keep aside. Bring milk to the boil and add trimoline. Cook until 70–80°C, remove and add to egg yolk mixture. Whisk non-stop on low heat until thickened.

· Split vanilla bean and scrape out seeds. Add vanilla seeds to milk mixture. Chill it down in the refrigerator and pour in cream and whisky. Churn in ice cream maker according to manufacturer's instructions.

Tuile

· Mix butter and confectioner's sugar together, followed by egg white and flour. Whiskuntil it becomes a paste.

· To make tuile, use a cardboard stencil with a 24 x 2-cm rectangular cut-out. Place stencil on a baking tray. Spread paste evenly on stencil with a palette knife.

· Roast in the oven for 5–6 minutes at 180°C until golden brown. Lift the stencil when still warm to get tuile, wind tuile around the handle of a rolling pin and leave to set. Once cooled, keep in airtight container with a packet of food-safe silica gel.

Berry Compote

· Cook berries gently in castor sugar and water until broken down.

· Serve bread and butter pudding topped with tuile, ice cream and berry compote. Garnish with mint leaf.

BREAD AND BUTTER PUDDING

Dehydrated Berries Bread and Butter Pudding with Whisky Ice Cream

6
-
C
O
U
R
S
E

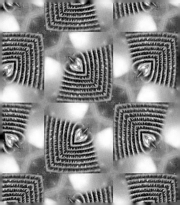

CAULIFLOWER ESPUMA
Cauliflower Espuma with Sevruga Caviar

YIELDS 500 ML

INGREDIENTS

Cauliflower Purée

Onion	50 g, peeled and chopped
Unsalted butter	40 g
Olive oil	30 ml
Cauliflower	250 g, cut into small florets
Thyme	1 g
Bay leaf	1
Chicken stock	100 ml
	(see Basic Techniques pg 174)
Cream	80 ml
Salt and pepper	a pinch
Sevruga caviar	30 g

Garnishing

Chives	a few sticks

METHOD

Cauliflower Purée

· Sweat onion with butter and olive oil until soft. Add cauliflower and sauté for another 5 minutes. Add thyme, bay leaf and chicken stock. Bring to the boil and simmer for 20 minutes. Add cream and reduce further for another 5 minutes. Season to taste.

· Remove bay leaf and blend mixture in a food processor. Pass blended mixture through a fine sieve and chill it down immediately in a blast chiller or refrigerator. Transfer into a foamer, filling up halfway. Charge up foamer with one charger and shake until a mousse-like consistency is achieved. If it is too thin, give it a few more shakes until it becomes firmer.

· Pipe cauliflower espuma into shot glasses. Top with Sevruga caviar and garnish with chives.

SALAD OF SWEET WATER MARRON

**Salad of Sweet Water Marron with Honey Tomato,
Mesclun Salad and Japanese Whitebait Crisp "Tatami Iwashi"**

YIELDS 4 SERVINGS

INGREDIENTS

Marrons

Marrons	4
Court bouillon	1 recipe
	(see Basic Techniques pg 174)

Salad

Honey tomato	4, cut into halves
Mesclun salad	100 g
Edible flowers	

Tomato Dressing

Fresh tomato purée	30 ml
Olive oil	100 ml
Red chilli	3 g, brunoise
Lemon zest	1 g
Lemon juice	10 ml
Chives	2 g, chopped
Tarragon	1 g, chopped
Chervil	2 g, chopped
Salt and pepper	a pinch

Garnishing

Whitebait crisp	4 sheets, baked until crispy

METHOD

Marrons

- Plunge marrons into court bouillon for 5–7 minutes, depending on the size of marrons used. When cooked, shock marrons in ice-cold water to prevent further cooking. Remove heads and shell marrons. Cut into halves lengthwise and refrigerate before use.

Tomato Dressing

- Combine all the tomato dressing ingredients except salt and pepper together in a mixing bowl with a whisk, stirring briskly until all the ingredients are well mixed and emulsified. Season to taste.

- Serve marrons with salad and drizzle with tomato dressing. Garnish with Japanese whitebait crisp.

CHILEAN SEA BASS

Chilean Sea Bass with Ginger Tomato Sauce and Crispy *Jin Hwa* Ham

YIELDS 4 SERVINGS

INGREDIENTS

Chilean Sea Bass

Chilean Sea Bass fillets	4, 60 g each, skinned
Salt and pepper	a pinch
Butter	20 ml
Olive oil	20 g

Ginger Tomato Sauce

Olive oil	40 ml
Garlic	10 g, peeled and chopped
Red onion	40 g, peeled and chopped
Young ginger	5 g, peeled and grated
Lemon grass	5 g, finely chopped
Roma tomato	250 g, skinned and diced
Fish sauce	10 ml
Lime juice	5 ml
Granulated sugar	10 g
Salt and pepper	a pinch
Coriander leaves	5 g, chopped

Garnishing

Jin Hwa Ham (Chinese air-dried ham)	a few strips, crisp-fried
Curry leaves	4, deep-fried

METHOD

Chilean Sea Bass

- Season Chilean sea bass with salt and pepper. Heat butter and olive oil and sauté sea bass on medium heat until golden brown on both sides.

Ginger Tomato Sauce

- Heat olive oil and sauté garlic, onion, ginger and lemon grass until soft. Add tomato, fish sauce, lime juice and sugar. Simmer for 10 minutes. Season to taste. Add chopped coriander leaves just before serving.

- Serve sea bass with tomato sauce. Garnish with julienne of *Jin Hwa* ham and curry leaf.

GREEN PEA CAPPUCCINO
Green Pea Cappuccino with Green Tea Sorbet

YIELDS 1 LITRE GREEN PEA SOUP AND 1.3
LITRES GREEN TEA SORBET

INGREDIENTS

Green Pea Soup

White onion	50 g, diced
Smoked bacon	30 g
Olive oil	30 ml
Thyme	2 g
Chicken stock	700 ml
	(see Basic Techniques pg 174)
Frozen green peas	300 g
Salt and pepper	a pinch
Milk	200 ml

Green Tea Sorbet

Sugar syrup	1 litre
	(see Basic Techniques pg 174)
Green tea powder	15 g
Lemon juice	15 ml

Garnishing

Wasabi-coated dried green peas	ground into powder with spice grinder

METHOD

Green Pea Soup

- Sweat onion and smoked bacon in olive oil. Add thyme and chicken stock. Simmer until onions are soft. Add in green peas and bring to the boil then chill it down immediately.

- Remove smoked bacon and blend soup in commercial blender and pass through a fine sieve. Season to taste. Fill up three-quarters of a shot glass.

- Bring milk to just before boiling point. Use a handheld electric blender and blend until foamy. Scoop cappuccino foam onto soup. Sprinkle with green pea powder.

Green Tea Sorbet

- Bring syrup to the boil. Add in green tea powder and lemon juice. Chill and churn in ice cream maker according to manufacturer's instructions to sorbet consistency.

- Serve green pea cappuccino with green tea sorbet. Sprinkle green pea powder on cappuccino.

INGREDIENTS

Lamb Shank

Lamb shank, on bone	4, 160 g each
Salt and pepper	to taste
Paprika	a pinch
Mirepoix	80 g
	(see Glossary pg 172)
Hoisin sauce	30 ml
Lamb stock	1 litre
	(see Basic Techniques pg 174)
Red wine	150 ml
Coriander seeds	3 g, toasted
Arrowroot starch	for thickening
Parsnips	4

Chanterelle

Fresh Chanterelle mushrooms	80 g, trimmed
Olive oil	20 ml
Salt and pepper	a pinch
Dry white wine	20 ml
Baby carrots	4, peeled and trimmed
Pencil asparagus	4 spears, peeled and trimmed
Salt and pepper	a pinch
La Ratte potatoes	4, steamed and peeled

Garnishing

Flat parsley	a few sprigs

METHOD

Lamb Shank

- Season lamb shank with salt, pepper and a pinch of paprika. Sear in a pan at medium heat to seal all sides.

- Remove from heat. Sauté mirepoix until lightly brown and mix with lamb shank in a pot. Add hoisin sauce, lamb stock, red wine and coriander seeds. Cover with lid and braise in oven at 160°C for 1 hour 45 minutes.

- Reserve braising liquid. Thicken with arrowroot starch and reduce to make lamb jus reduction.

- Lamb shank should be tender and you should be able to remove bone from meat easily.

- Trim parsnip to 12-cm length and 1.5-cm diameter. Season with salt and pepper. Blanch then sauté at high heat until soft and browned on all sides. Remove the shank bone and push parsnip "bone" into lamb shank.

Chanterelle

- Lightly sauté Chanterelle mushrooms with olive oil. Season and then deglaze with dry white wine. Blanch asparagus and baby carrot then lightly sauté with olive oil. Season with salt and pepper.

- Slice La Ratte potato at 0.5-cm thickness and serve with lamb shank with vegetables and lamb jus reduction. Garnish with parsley.

BRAISED LAMB SHANK
Braised Lamb Shank with Parsnip "Bone", Chanterelle Mushrooms and La Ratte Potato

YIELDS 2 LITRES ICE CREAM

INGREDIENTS

Earl Grey Tea Ice Cream

Cream	500 g
Milk	1 litre
Earl Grey tea leaves	35 g
Egg yolks	320 g
Castor sugar	200 g
Trimoline	180 g
Stabilizer	12 g

Churros

Butter	150 g
Water	300 ml
Plain (all-purpose) flour	150 g, sifted
Eggs	3
Egg yolk	1
Oil	for deep-frying
Castor sugar	100 g
Ground cinnamon	a pinch

METHOD

Earl Grey Tea Ice Cream

· Bring cream and milk to the boil together. Add Earl Grey tea leaves and infuse for 30 minutes. Strain.

· Bring cream and milk to the boil again and pour over egg yolks and sugar. Return to the stove and cook until 85°C. Cool down and add trimoline and stabilizer. Churn in ice cream maker according to manufacturer's instructions.

Churros

· Bring butter and water to the boil. Pour in flour and stir with a wooden spoon to make sure that it is fully incorporated. There should not be any lumps. Turn off fire.

· Use a k-beater to blend slowly first then turn up speed. Add eggs and egg yolk. Blend until fully incorporated.

· Transfer to a piping bag with a star nozzle.

· Heat up a pot of oil until hot. Pipe churros paste into oil and snip off an appropriate length with scissors. Deep-fry until golden brown. Drain excess oil and sprinkle with sugar and ground cinnamon.

· Serve Earl Grey tea ice cream with churros.

EARL GREY TEA
Earl Grey Tea Ice Cream with Churros
ICE CREAM

7
-
C
O
U
R
S
E

SEARED SCALLOP

Seared Scallop with Chilli Kalamansi Lime Salsa on *Kaiware* Sprouts

INGREDIENTS

Seared Scallop

Scallops	4
Salt and pepper	a pinch
Kaiware sprouts	12 g

Chilli Kalamansi Lime Salsa

Olive oil	100 ml
Red chilli	5 g, brunoise
Kalamansi lime	5 g, pip removed and finely chopped
Semi-dried tomato	60 g, diced
Coriander leaves	5 g, chopped
Shallots	20 g, peeled and chopped
Garlic	5 g, peeled and chopped
Salt and pepper	a pinch
Palm sugar (*gula Melaka*)	to taste

METHOD

Seared Scallop

• Season scallop with salt and pepper. Sear each side on high heat for 30 seconds.

Chilli Kalamansi Lime Salsa

• Mix all the chilli kalamansi lime salsa ingredients together. Season to taste.

• Serve seared scallop with *kaiware* sprouts and salsa.

GIZZARD SHAD "KOHADA"

Escabeche of Gizzard Shad "Kohada"

INGREDIENTS

Marinated Gizzard Shad	8 fillets

Escabeche

Shallots	50 g, peeled and sliced
Baby carrot	100 g, peeled and sliced
Young fennel	100 g, sliced
Olive oil	50 ml
White wine vinegar or verjuice	40 ml
Coriander seeds	1 g, toasted and lightly crushed
Fennel seeds	1 g, toasted and lightly crushed
Sugar	to taste
Water	100 ml
Salt	to taste
Coriander leaves	3 g, chopped
Aged balsamic vinegar	20 ml

METHOD

Escabeche

- Sweat sliced shallots, carrots and fennel in olive oil until soft. Deglaze with white wine vinegar or verjuice. Add in coriander and fennel seeds.

- Add sugar and water and reduce. Simmer until half of the liquid is absorbed by the vegetables. Season to taste and add chopped coriander leaves.

- Pour warm escabeche over fish fillets. Refrigerate overnight to marinate.

- Serve fish fillets and escabeche with aged balsamic vinegar.

INGREDIENTS

Sautéed Foie Gras

Goose Foie Gras	4 slices, 60 g each
Plain (all-purpose) flour	for dusting

Tomato Tart

Ready-made puff pastry dough	200 g
Onion confit*	80 g
Oven-dried tomato wedges	16

Garnishing

Port wine and balsamic reduction	a few spoons
(see Basic Techniques pg 174)	
Extra virgin olive oil	
Sea salt	a pinch
Freshly cracked black peppercorn	a pinch
Gold leaf (optional)	

METHOD

Sautéed Foie Gras

• Sprinkle both sides of foie gras with flour. Sauté over medium-high heat, until golden brown.

Tomato Tart

• Roll the puff pastry dough out to 3-mm thickness. Using a round pastry cutter, cut out 4 tart shapes of diameter 7-cm.

• Brush with eggwash. Prick holes with fork and bake blind for 5–7 minutes at 180°C, until browned. Leave aside.

• Spread onion confit on tart. Top with oven-dried tomato. Return to oven to keep warm.

• Serve foie gras on tomato tart. Serve with port wine and balsamic reduction and sprinkle a few drops of extra virgin olive oil. Sprinkle with sea salt and freshly cracked black peppercorn. Garnish with gold leaf (optional).

Onion Confit*

White onion	400 g, peeled and sliced
Goose fat	50 ml
Chicken stock	80 ml
(see Basic Techniques pg 174)	
Thyme	2 g, chopped
Salt and pepper	a pinch

• Sauté sliced onion in goose fat until browned. Add a bit of chicken stock and thyme, making sure that chicken stock is well absorbed by onion.

SAUTÉED FOIE GRAS WITH
TOMATO TART

Sautéed Foie Gras with Tomato Tart, Port and Balsamic Reduction

INGREDIENTS

Oriental Herb and Chilli Linguini

Linguini	120 g
Red chilli	8 g, sliced
Fish sauce	10 ml
Mint leaves	4 g
Basil leaves	4 g
Coriander leaves	4 g
Spring onion (scallion)	4 g, julienned
Olive oil	20 ml
Salt and pepper	a pinch

Salmon in Lemon Grass Skewer

Salmon fillets	8, 30 g each
Lemon grass skewers	8
Young ginger	20 g, peeled and minced
Lemon grass	20 g, minced
Lime juice	20 ml
Lime zest	3 g
Canola oil	30 ml
Mirin	60 ml
Soy sauce, low sodium	70 ml

METHOD

Oriental Herb and Chilli Linguini

· Cook linguini until al dente. Toss with sliced red chilli, fish sauce, mint, basil and coriander leaves, spring onion and olive oil. Season to taste.

Salmon in Lemon Grass Skewer

· Use a bamboo skewer to pierce through salmon. Remove then replace with lemon grass skewer.

· Combine minced ginger, minced lemon grass, lime juice, lime zest, sunflower oil, *mirin* and soy sauce to make ginger *mirin* soy sauce. Marinate salmon with sauce.

· Drain off excess marinade. Sear salmon over medium heat, making sure that it is still pink in the middle.

· Serve salmon with linguini.

ORIENTAL HERB AND
Oriental Herb and Chilli Linguini with Seared Salmon in Lemon Grass Skewer
CHILLI LINGUINI

CHILLED BEETROOT SOUP

Chilled Beetroot Soup with Crème Fraîche and Fried Cheese Dumpling

INGREDIENTS

Beetroot Soup

Beetroot	150 g, peeled and diced
Red onion	50 g, peeled and diced
Thyme	2 g
Mace	a pinch, optional
Red wine vinegar	20 ml
Water	400 ml
Salt and sugar	a pinch
Vodka	10 ml

Fried Cheese Dumplings

Goat cheese	120 g
Ricotta cheese	240 g
Semolina flour	240 g
Egg whites	2
Plain (all-purpose) flour	120 g
Baking powder	2.5 g
Salt	2 g
Sugar	100 g

Garnishing

Crème fraîche	a few dollops
Fried sage	
Gold leaf (optional)	
Olive oil	

METHOD

Beetroot Soup

- Cook all the ingredients for about 40 minutes, until soft, on simmering heat.

- Blend in a food processor until smooth. Season to taste.

Fried Cheese Dumplings

- Combine all the ingredients and use a K-beater to form dough. Roll it in your palm into small balls. Deep-fry until golden brown.

- Serve soup with a dollop of crème fraîche and a dumpling. Garnish with fried sage and gold leaf (optional). Drizzle a few drops of olive oil.

LAMB TENDERLOIN

Truffle-crusted Lamb Tenderloin with Pinot Noir Sauce and Green Pea Purée

YIELDS 4 SERVINGS

INGREDIENTS

Olive oil	500 ml
Garlic	5 cloves, lightly smashed with skin on
Lemon rind	1
Rosemary	a few sprigs
Thyme	a few sprigs
Whole black peppercorns	20
Lamb tenderloin	240 g
Black truffles	20 g, chopped
Chives	30 g, chopped
Freshly ground black peppercorn	a pinch
Sea salt	a pinch

Green Pea Purée

Onion	100 g, peeled and chopped
Unsalted butter	50 g
Thyme	2 g
Chicken stock	80 ml
	(see Basic Techniques pg 174)
Frozen green peas	300 g
Salt and pepper	a pinch

Green Pea Emulsion

Green pea purée	30 g
Milk	200 ml

Pinot Noir Sauce

Shallots	50 g, peeled and sliced
Port wine	100 ml
Pinot Noir	100 ml
Lamb jus	500 ml
	(see Basic Techniques pg 174)

Garnishing

Fresh green peas	20 g, blanched

METHOD

Lamb Tenderloin

· Infuse olive oil with whole garlic, lemon rind, rosemary, thyme and whole peppercorn. Heat until 70˚C.

· Add lamb tenderloin and poach in oil for 4–5 minutes until medium-rare and pink in the middle. Let it rest before cutting.

· Garnish with chopped truffles, chopped chives, freshly ground black pepper and sea salt.

Green Pea Purée

· Sauté onion with butter, without colouring. Add thyme and chicken stock. Simmer until onion is very soft.

· Add in frozen green peas, bring to the boil and blend in a food processor until smooth. Season to taste. Pass through a fine sieve.

Green Pea Emulsion

· Mix warm milk with purée. Blend with handheld blender until frothy.

Pinot Noir Sauce

· Cook shallots in Pinot Noir and port wine. Reduce until syrupy. Add lamb jus and reduce further until it coats the back of a spoon. Strain sauce through a fine sieve.

· Serve lamb tenderloin with some fresh peas and green pea emulsion. Finish with Pinot Noir sauce.

INGREDIENTS

Ready-made filo pastry	250 g

Cream Cheese

Goat cheese	100 g
Blue cheese	100 g
Ricotta cheese	200 g
Egg yolk	1
Freshly cracked black peppercorn	a pinch

Basil Ice Cream

Basil leaves	100 g
Parsley	40 g
Milk	1 litre
Cream	500 g
Stabilizer	10 g
Trimoline	180 g
Castor sugar	180 g

Garnishing

Gold leaf (optional)	
Pistachio nuts	
Basil oil	
Fried basil leaves	4
Fresh figs	2, cut into quarters

METHOD

- Cut filo pastry into 12 pieces, 3.5 x 8-cm each.

- Bake in an oven at 150°C until golden brown. Leave aside.

Cream Cheese

- Mix all the ingredients together with a K-beater until evenly mixed and creamy. Leave in the refrigerator to chill for 2 hours.

Basil Ice Cream

- Blanch basil leaf and parsley. Plunge into ice-cold water to refresh. Drain and pat dry. Add milk and purée until fine in a blender.

- Refrigerate then add cream, stabilizer, trimoline and sugar. Churn in ice cream maker according to manufacturer's instructions.

- Transfer chilled cream cheese to a piping bag. Lay 1 piece of filo pastry down and pipe 1 layer of cream cheese onto it. Repeat with 2 more layers of filo pastry and cream cheese. Cap with 1 more piece of filo pastry. Garnish with a piece of gold leaf (optional).

- Serve mille feuille with pistachio nuts. Drizzle with basil oil. Serve a scoop of ice cream on top of pistachio nuts and Garnish with fried basil and fresh fig quarters.

MILLE FEUILLE
Mille Feuille of Cream Cheese with Basil Ice Cream

8-COURSE

YIELDS 4 SERVINGS

INGREDIENTS

Yabbies	8
Salt and pepper	a pinch

Sesame Soy Dressing

White sesame seeds	3 g, toasted
Sesame oil	50 ml
Canola oil	50 ml
Light soy sauce	40 ml
Chicken stock	50 ml
	(see Basic Techniques pg 174)
Lemon	1, juiced
Sugar	a pinch
Pickled ginger	10 g, finely chopped
Garlic	10 g, peeled and finely chopped

Garnishing

Golden mushroom	80 g
Crème fraîche	30 ml
Wasabi *tobiko*	12 g
Sansho leaves	4
Oba leaves	4

METHOD

· Steam yabbies for 4 minutes. Remove heads and shells, keeping tails intact.

Sesame Soy Dressing

· Combine all the ingredients in an airtight jar and shake vigorously to emulsify.

· Serve 2 yabbies with golden mushrooms and top with crème fraîche and wasabi *tobiko*. Garnish with *sansho* leaf. Drizzle some sesame soy dressing.

STEAMED YABBIES
Steamed Yabbies with Golden Mushroom and Sesame Soy Dressing

CARPACCIO OF TUNA "NIÇOISE"

Carpaccio of Tuna "Niçoise" with Balsamic and Basil Oil

INGREDIENTS

Tuna fillets	120 g
Quail eggs	2, hardboiled, shelled and halved
Haricot vert	24 g, blanched and cut into segments
Yellow frisée	a few sprigs
Niçoise olives	4
Honey tomatoes	4
Marche leaves	4
Anchovy fillets	4
La Ratte potato	8 slices

Garnishing

Basil oil	30 ml
Aged balsamic vinegar	30 ml

METHOD

· Freeze tuna loin until semi-hard. Slice it paper-thin with a commercial meat slicer.

· Line tuna fillets on plate, overlapping one another, to form a rectangle.

· Arrange quail egg half on haricot vert segments. Insert yellow frisée into olive. Arrange honey tomato on marche leaf and anchovy fillet on top of potato slice. Serve with basil oil and balsamic vinegar.

INGREDIENTS

Duck Breast

Duck breasts	2
Salt	a pinch
Freshly cracked black peppercorn	a pinch
Canola oil	10 ml
Oregano	2 g, chopped

Spice Grilled Plum

Plums	2, cut into halves and pitted
Spice sugar (95% granulated sugar and 5% ground cinnamon)	1 tsp
Spice honey* (honey laced with ground cinnamon and star anise)	50 ml
Raisins	30 g
Dried apricot	30 g, cut into small dices

Sauce

Port wine	100 ml
Shallots	30 g, peeled and sliced
Duck jus	300 ml
(see Basic Techniques pg 174)	
Spice honey*	1 tsp

Garnishing

Deep-fried *Oba* leaves	4

METHOD

Duck Breast

• Season duck breasts with salt, coarsely crushed black peppercorn and oil. Pan-fry, skin-side down, at low to medium heat to drain off excess fat.

• Cook slowly until golden brown. Turn over, sprinkle oregano on top and finish off in the oven at 140°C for 3–7 minutes, depending on the size of duck breast.

• Let the meat rest for 10 minutes before slicing.

Spice Grilled Plum

• Brush some butter over plum halves and sprinkle with spice sugar. Pan-fry until caramelised all over.

• Add spice honey and let it cook until it bubbles and honey turns dark brown. Remove from heat.

• Turn plum halves over and stuff with dried fruits. Pour excess honey over it and finish off in the oven at 140°C for 3 minutes.

Sauce

• Reduce port wine and shallots to one-third. Add duck jus and reduce further, until it coats the back of a spoon. Add spice honey and incorporate well.

• Serve duck breast slices with sauce and stuffed plum half. Garnish with deep-fried *Oba* leaf.

ROAST PEPPERED DUCK
Roast Peppered Duck Breast Slices with Spice Grilled Plum
BREAST SLICES

INGREDIENTS

Tomato Lentil Soup

Onion	100 g, peeled and chopped
Garlic	10 g, peeled and chopped
Cumin	3 g
Curry leaf	1 g
Red chilli	10 g, minced
Coriander root	20 g
Very ripe tomatoes	300 g, roughly chopped
Chicken stock	1.5 litres
	(see Basic Techniques pg 174)
Yellow lentils	100 g

Lentil Tuiles

Salt	45 g
Egg white	200 g
Butter	200 g, melted
Confectioner's sugar	100 g
Flat parsley	20 g
Toasted yellow lentils	100 g

Garnishing
Coriander leaves

METHOD

Tomato Lentil Soup

· Sauté onion, garlic, cumin and curry leaf until fragrant. Add red chilli, coriander root, tomatoes and chicken stock.

· Add yellow lentils and cook until they become very soft. Blend with a food processor and pass through a fine sieve.

· Bring back to the boil. Season to taste.

Lentil Tuiles

· Combine all the ingredients except the toasted lentils. Whisk until it becomes a paste.

· Use a cardboard stencil with a 24 x 2-cm rectangular cut-out. Place stencil on a baking tray and spread paste evenly over stencil with a palette knife. Sprinkle toasted lentils over the paste.

· Roast in the oven for 5–6 minutes at 180°C until golden brown. Once cooled, keep in airtight container with a packet of food-safe silica gel.

· Serve soup with lentil tuiles. Garnish with a sprig of coriander leaf.

TOMATO AND YELLOW

Tomato and Yellow Lentil Soup with Toasted Lentil Tuiles

LENTIL SOUP

PAN-ROASTED TURBOT

Pan-roasted Turbot with *Sugitake* Mushroom and *Edamame* Ragout

YIELDS 4 SERVINGS

INGREDIENTS

Pan-roasted Turbot

Turbot fillets	4, 80 g each
Olive oil	80 ml
Coarse sea salt	a pinch
Freshly cracked black peppercorn	a pinch

Mushroom and *Edamame* Ragout

Sugitake mushrooms	120 g
White wine	80 ml
Edamame beans	60 g, blanched and podded

Garnishing

Oven-dried Roma tomatoes	40 g
Chives	12 g, chopped
Extra virgin olive oil	120 ml
Lemon	1/2, juiced
Coarse sea salt	a pinch
Freshly cracked black peppercorn	a pinch

METHOD

Pan-roasted Turbot

· Brush turbot with olive oil and season with coarse sea salt and black pepper. Place the turbot fillet in a preheated broiler pan and cook until golden brown. Turn and finish cooking the fish in a preheated oven at 180°C. When the fish is three-quarters cooked, remove the pan from the oven. The heat generated from the broiler pan should continue to cook the fish through.

Mushroom and *Edamane* Ragout

· In the meantime, sauté the *Sugitake* mushrooms for just under 2 minutes and deglaze with white wine. Cook further until white wine dissipates; then add *edamame* and season to taste.

· Serve pan-roasted turbot on mushroom and *edamame* ragout. Garnish with oven-dried tomatoes and chopped chives and drizzle with extra virgin olive oil. Lightly squeeze a few drops of lemon juice over and sprinkle with coarse sea salt and black peppercorn.

GINGER LYCHEE GRANITÉ

Ginger Lychee Granité

INGREDIENTS

Fresh lychee juice	1.5 litres, made from 500 g fresh lychee pulp and 1 litre sugar syrup
	(see Basic Techniques pg 174)
Lemon juice	100 ml
Ginger juice	100 ml

Japanese pickled ginger (*gari*)
Fresh lychees   skinned and stoned

METHOD

• Purée fresh lychee pulp with sugar syrup in a food processor.

• Add lime juice and ginger juice. Mix well then strain through a fine sieve.

• Leave in a shallow bowl in a freezer. When ice crystals start forming around the edges, scrape surface with a fork to incorporate ice. Continue freezing and scraping every 30–40 minutes, for 4 hours.

• Stuff a seeded fresh lychee with *gari*.

• Serve granité with stuffed ginger lychee.

BRAISED BEEF BLADE
Braised Beef Blade with Blue Cheese Polenta and Roasted Root Vegetables

INGREDIENTS

Braised Beef Blade

Beef blade	4 portions, 120 g each
	(40% weight loss usually occurs)
Salt and pepper	a pinch
Mirepoix	100 g
	(see Glossary pg 172)
Garlic	10 cloves, with skin on
Thyme	2 g, chopped
Rosemary	2 g, chopped
Orange peel	optional
Tomato paste	40 g
Red wine	100 ml
Veal stock	1 litre
	(see Basic Techniques pg 174)
Arrowroot starch	for thickening

Blue Cheese Polenta

Milk	1 litre
Onion	80 g, peeled and chopped
Garlic	20 g, peeled and chopped
Bay leaves	2
Thyme	0.5 g
Rosemary	0.5 g
Polenta flour	110 g
Unsalted butter	30 g, cubed
Blue cheese	30 g
Salt and pepper	a pinch

Roasted Root Vegetables

Baby carrot	4, trimmed
Parsnip	20 g, blanched
Red onion	1, peeled and cut into wedges
Baby beetroot	1, peeled and cut into quarters
Garlic	4 bulbs
Olive oil	30 ml
Rosemary	1 g, chopped
Thyme	1 g, chopped
Salt and pepper	a pinch

Garnishing

Flat parsley	4 sprigs

METHOD

Braised Beef Blade

- Tie beef blade firmly with butcher's meat string at 2-cm intervals. This will help the beef blade retain its shape even after cooking while preventing excessive shrinkage. Season beef blade with salt and pepper. Sear over medium-high heat until browned all around.

- In the same pan, prepare braising liquid. Sauté mirepoix, garlic thyme, rosemary and orange peel until lightly caramelised. Add tomato paste and stir.

- Deglaze pan with red wine. Reduce to two-thirds. Add veal stock.

- Transfer beef blade to braising liquid. Cover and braise in oven at 160°C for 2 hours.

- Let the meat cool down for 10 minutes before removing the butcher's string and cutting into serving portions. Return beef blade to braising liquid and reheat until ready to serve.

- Pour part of braising liquid through a fine sieve. Reduce then add arrowroot starch to thicken. Keep sauce aside.

Blue Cheese Polenta

- Bring milk, onion, garlic, bay leaves, thyme and rosemary to the boil. Simmer for 10 minutes and steep for 20 minutes. Strain milk through a fine sieve and bring to the boil. Add polenta flour and stir constantly until cooked but still runny. You may need to add in more milk to keep the polenta soft.

- Finish off with a few cold butter cubes and blue cheese. Mix well. Season to taste.

Roasted Root Vegetables

- Marinate and toss with olive oil, thyme, rosemary, salt and pepper. Roast in the oven at 160°C for 10–12 minutes, or until just cooked.

- Serve beef blade on a circular base of polenta. Top with roasted root vegetables. Serve with a spoonful of sauce.

COCONUT SAGO SOUP
Coconut Sago Soup with Kamquat-melon Dumpling and Berries

YIELDS 4 SERVINGS

INGREDIENTS

Coconut Sago Soup

Water	2 litres
Sago pearls	120 g
Rock melon juice	240 ml
Sugar syrup	to taste
	(see Basic Techniques pg 174)
Coconut cream	240 ml

Kamquat-melon Dumpling

Kamquat compote*	40 g
Rock melon	40 g, brunoise
Mint leaves	a few, julienned
Wanton wrappers	4
Rock melon balls	8
Fresh blackberries	8
Fresh raspberries	12
Fresh blueberries	12
Cherries	4
Mint leaves	a few sprigs

METHOD

Coconut Sago Soup

· Bring water to the boil. Add in sago pearls and cook until sago pearls look translucent with specks within.

· Turn off fire and let sago cook for 1–2 minutes until completely translucent. Strain and soak in cold water until cooled. Drain off water completely.

· Blend rock melon juice and add sugar syrup until desired sweetness. Mix rock melon juice with coconut cream. Add in sago pearls. Keep chilled.

Kamquat-melon Dumpling

· Mix kamquat compote with melon brunoise and mint leaves. Place 1 teaspoon of filling at the centre of wanton wrapper. Moisten edges of wrapper and fold wrapper over the filling, forming a triangle. Press edges firmly to seal.

· Bring water to the boil. Cook dumplings for 3 minutes. Scoop up and plunge into cold water until cooled.

· Serve coconut sago soup with dumplings and fruits. Garnish with mint leaves.

Kamquat Compote*

Vanilla bean	1
Kamquat	200 g, sliced
Honey	120 g
Red wine vinegar	30 ml

· Split vanilla bean and scrape out the seeds.

· Cook kamquat with honey, vanilla seeds and red wine vinegar very gently for 20–30 minutes until syrupy. Cool and refrigerate.

9 - C O U R S E

BELON OYSTER
Belon Oyster with Kalamansi Lime Granité

YIELDS 4 SERVINGS

INGREDIENTS

Belon oysters	4, freshly shucked
Kalamansi lime juice	150 ml
Sugar syrup	100 ml
	(see Basic Techniques pg 174)
Tabasco sauce	a few drops
Kalamansi limes	2, cut into halves

METHOD

· Combine Kalamansi lime juice and syrup. Mix well and leave in freezer until frozen.

· Scrape the surface with a fork to form ice crystals and freeze again for 4 hours.

· Serve oyster with a scoop of Kalamansi lime granité and a Kalamansi lime half. Drizzle 1–2 drops of Tabasco sauce on oyster.

CHILLED SILKEN TOFU

Chilled Silken Tofu Medallions with Sevruga Caviar, Capelin Roe and Wasabi *Tobiko*

MEDALLIONS

YIELDS 4 SERVINGS

INGREDIENTS

Sevruga caviar	40 g
Capelin roe	40 g
Wasabi *Tobiko*	40 g
Silken tofu, preferably in cylindrical shape	500 g

Garnishing

Chives	4 sticks, 6–7 cm in length

METHOD

· Cut the silken tofu into 12 pieces with a pastry cutter 3-cm in diameter and 2-cm in height.

· Top each silken tofu with 3 different types of fish roe and garnish with chive sticks. Serve chilled.

INGREDIENTS

Tomato Essence

Tomato	500 g, sun-ripened
Celery	100 g
Basil leaves	20 g
Water	100 ml
Tabasco sauce	to taste
Worcestershire sauce	1 tsp
Salt and sugar	to taste

Dumpling

Langoustine	50 g, roughly chopped
Scallop	50 g, roughly chopped
Basil leaves	3 g, julienned
Salt and pepper	to taste
Wanton wrappers	8, of diameter 8-cm

Basil Oil

Basil leaves	a few
Parsley	20 g
Olive oil	200 ml
Salt	a pinch

Garnishing

Ligurian olives	4
Young basil leaves	a few sprigs
Tomato dices	20 g

METHOD

Tomato Essence

- Coarsely blend tomato, celery and basil leaves in a food processar. Transfer to a pot and add water. Simmer until reduced by half.

- Strain through a fine sieve lined with a coffee filter. Bring it back to the boil and slowly simmer. Add a dash of Tabasco and Worcestershire sauce. Season to taste.

Dumpling

- Mix all the ingredients except wanton wrappers in a bowl. Scoop 8 g of this filling and place in the centre of a wanton wrapper. Fold wrapper over filling into a semi-circle and wet edges to seal.

- Line a bamboo steamer with a banana leaf, brushed with oil to prevent sticking. Steam dumplings for 1–2 minutes.

Basil Oil

- Purée basil, parsley, oil and salt in a food processor. Let it rest for 2–3 hours. Strain through a fine sieve lined with a coffee filter. Let it drip naturally for half a day.

- Serve dumplings with olives, a few springs of young basil leaves and tomato dices. Drizzle a few drops of basil oil.

Langoustine and Scallop Dumpling with Tomato Essence, Olives and Basil

BRANDADE DE MORUE

Brandade de Morue with Potato Chips

YIELDS 1 KG BRANDADE

INGREDIENTS

Brandade

Salted cod	250 g
Milk	1 litre
Thyme	1 g
Bay leaf	1
Olive oil	80 ml
Garlic confit	20 g
(see Basic Techniques pg 174)	
Lemon juice	15 ml
Mashed potato	200 g

Potato Chips

Potatoes	1–2
Clarified butter	100 ml
(see Basic Techniques pg 174)	
Fresh tarragon	a few sprigs
Extra virgin olive oil	for drizzling

METHOD

Brandade

· Soak cod in a pot of water overnight to get rid of salt content. Change water every few hours. Transfer cod to colander and strain off water.

· Cook cod in milk with thyme and bay leaf. Slowly poach until almost disintegrated. Drain and remove the bones and skin.

· Transfer cod, garlic confit, lemon juice and mashed potato to a blender. Slowly add olive oil and blend at medium speed to emulsify. This should be done in stages. The brandade should be light and airy. Season to taste.

Potato Chips

· Peel potatoes and trim them into long oval shapes. Using a Japanese mandolin, cut the potato into paper-thin slices. Sandwich a tarragon leaf inbetween 2 potato slices. Press and remove any air pockets between the 2 potato slices. Sandwich the potato chip between silpats and bake at 150°C for at least 20 minutes or until golden brown.

· Transfer brandade to a piping bag. Pipe into teacups and serve with potato chips. Drizzle a bit of extra virgin olive oil.

INGREDIENTS

Salmon

Salmon darne	4, 40 g each
Goose fat	500 ml

Puy Lentil Salad

Puy lentils	60 g
Chicken stock	300 ml
(see Basic Techniques pg 174)	
Bouquet-garni	50 g
(see Glossary pg 172)	
Olive oil	40 ml
Kenya beans	40 g
Red capsicum	40 g, diced
Green peas	20 g

Kaffir Lime Emulsion

Unsalted butter	30 g
Onion	60 g, peeled and chopped
Lemon grass	40 g, lightly smashed
Kaffir lime leaves	4
White wine	200 ml
Fish stock	300 ml
(see Basic Techniques pg 174)	
Cream	80 ml
Milk	50 ml

Garnishing

Salt and pepper	a pinch
Kaffir lime zest	

METHOD

Salmon

- Cook the salmon in goose fat at 65°C. Do not overheat the goose fat because the fish will sweat and white protein will form on the fish. The fish should still look pink even after cooking.

Puy Lentil Salad

- Boil lentils for 20–25 minutes in chicken stock with bouquet-garni.

- Drain off excess stock. Transfer lentil to mixing bowl. Add olive oil and the rest of the ingredients. Season to taste.

Kaffir Lime Emulsion

- Heat butter and sweat onion, lemon grass and kaffir lime leaves until fragrant. Add white wine and reduce to one-third. Add fish stock and reduce further for another 10 minutes.

- Add cream and milk. Cook for another 5 minutes. Pass through a fine sieve. Blend with a handheld blender.

- Arrange salmon on top of warm puy lentil salad. Serve with kaffir lime emulsion and kaffir lime zest.

CONFIT OF SALMON

Confit of Salmon with Warm Puy Lentil Salad and a Light Kaffir Lime Emulsion

YIELDS 1 LITRE

INGREDIENTS

Mangosteen Sorbet

Mangosteen pulp	500 ml
Sugar syrup	500 ml
	(see Basic Techniques pg 174)
Lemon juice	150 ml

Blueberry Coulis

Fresh blueberries	250 g
Sugar	80 g

METHOD

Mangosteen Sorbet

· Add mangosteen pulp to sugar syrup and lemon juice. Purée in a blender.

· Churn in ice cream maker according to manufacturer's instructions.

· Keep in freezer for 4 hours before serving.

Blueberry Coulis

· Purée fresh blueberry with sugar in a blender.

· Serve with a base of blueberry coulis and top with a scoop of sorbet. Garnish with a blueberry and a mangosteen wedge.

MANGOSTEEN SORBET

Mangosteen Sorbet

INGREDIENTS

Poached Beef Tenderloin

Beef tenderloin	400 g, trimmed
Beef stock	2 litres
	(see Basic Techniques pg 174)
Arrowroot starch	1 tsp
Butter	25 g

Pearl Barley Risotto

Onions	10 g, brunoise
Carrots	15 g, brunoise
Celery	10 g, brunoise
Baby leek	20 g, sliced diagonally
Air-dried beef	10 g, brunoise
Chicken stock	600 ml
	(see Basic Techniques pg 174)
Pearl barley	100 g, half-cooked
Unsalted butter	50 g

Garnishing

Sea salt

METHOD

Poached Beef Tenderloin

· Poach beef in beef stock until medium-rare. Remove and let it rest for 10 minutes. Portion. It should be pink in the middle.

· Thicken 200 ml beef stock with arrowroot starch and butter to make a very light sauce. Set aside.

Pearl Barley Risotto

· Sweat onions, carrots and celery. Add in baby leek and air-dried beef with chicken stock.

· Add in half-cooked barley. Cook for another 10 minutes, until all the chicken stock is absorbed. Add in butter to enhance the flavour.

· Serve poached beef with pearl barley risotto. Sprinkle some sea salt and spoon sauce around.

POACHED BEEF
Poached Beef Tenderloin with Pearl Barley Risotto
TENDERLOIN

INGREDIENTS

Brie Cheese Parcel

Ready-made filo pastry	12 sheets, each 12-cm square
Unsalted butter	100 g, melted
Spice sugar (95% granulated sugar and 5% ground cinnamon)	
Brie cheese	120 g
Macadamia nuts	40 g, toasted and roughly chopped

Spiced Honey Sauce

Butter	25 g
Honey	120 ml
Ground cinnamon	a pinch
Star anise	a pinch
Nutmeg	a pinch
Confectioner's sugar	10 g

METHOD

Brie Cheese Parcel

· Brush 3 sheets of filo pastry with melted butter. Sprinkle with spice sugar on the first sheet and lay second sheet on top. Rotate second sheet clockwise by 45° and sprinkle spice sugar. Lay third sheet on top in the same position as the first sheet and sprinkle spice sugar.

· Place 30 g of Brie cheese and 10 g of macadamia nuts on top of third sheet. Gather all the corners of pastry sheets and twist to tighten into a parcel.

Spiced Honey Sauce

· Bring butter and honey to the boil in a saucepan. Sprinkle ground cinnamon and star anise. Simmer until thick and syrupy.

· Bake in the oven at 160°C for 5–7 minutes until golden brown. Dust some confectioner's sugar and serve parcel in a pool of spiced honey sauce on a plate and complement with a whole macadamia nut.

BRIE CHEESE PARCEL

Brie Cheese Parcel with Spiced Honey and Macadamia Nut Sauce

INGREDIENTS

Chocolate Tuiles

Butter	100 g, softened
Confectioner's sugar	100 g
Cocoa powder	40 g
Egg white	115 g
Plain (all-purpose) flour	85 g, sifted

Trio of Chocolate Ice Cream

Milk	750 ml
Sugar	70 g
Milk powder	45 g
White chocolate, milk chocolate and dark chocolate	280 g each, chopped
Cream	250 ml
Stabilizer	6 g
Trimoline	90 g

Poached Cherries

Port wine	750 ml
Dark cherries	250 g, pitted and halved

METHOD

Chocolate Tuiles

· Mix butter, confectioner's sugar, cocoa powder, egg white and flour with an electric mixer until smooth. Refrigerate for at least 3 hours.

· Spread the mixture very thinly on a silpat and bake in an oven at 180°C for 5 minutes or until light golden brown. Leave to cool on a sheet of silicon paper.

Trio of Chocolate Ice Cream

· Bring 750 ml milk, 70 g sugar and 45 g milk powder to a simmer at 80°C in a saucepan. Remove from heat and add the chopped white chocolate. Stir until completely melted. When lukewarm, add 250 ml cream, 6 g stabilizer and 90 g trimoline, and churn in an ice cream maker according to manufacturer's instructions. Repeat for milk and dark chocolate. When making dark chocolate ice cream, add 50 g of cocoa powder.

Poached Cherries

· In a saucepan, reduce the port wine until thick and syrupy. Add the dark cherries and cook for another 3 minutes. Remove from heat and chill in the refrigerator.

· Serve trio of chocolate ice cream with chocolate tuiles and poached cherries in port wine.

CHOCOLATE ICE CREAM
Chocolate Ice Cream Sandwich with Poached Cherries in Port Wine
SANDWICH

10
-
C
O
U
R
S
E

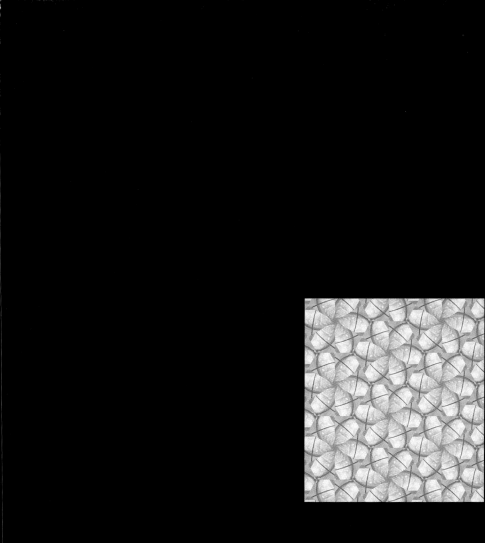

STEAMED LA RATTE POTATO

Steamed La Ratte Potato with Sour Cream and Golden Oscietra Caviar

INGREDIENTS

La Ratte potatoes	4, 30 g each
Sour cream	60 ml
Golden Oscietra caviar	40 g
Chives	4 sticks

METHOD

· Steam La Ratte potatoes until just cooked. Peel off skin and slice potato at 5-mm thickness.

· Serve a stack of potato slices, topped with sour cream and caviar. Garnish with chive stick.

GREEN TEA SOBA NOODLES

Red Legged Prawns on Green Tea *Soba* Noodles with Sesame *Miso* Dressing

YIELDS 4 SERVINGS

INGREDIENTS

Red legged prawns	4, steamed
Green tea *soba* noodles	80 g, cooked
Hon Shimeji mushroom	24 g, lightly sautéed
Chives	2 g, chopped

Sesame *Miso* Dressing

Sesame paste or Tahini	15 g
White *miso* paste, low sodium	90 g
Lemon juice	10 ml
Rice wine vinegar	10 ml
Ginger juice	20 ml
Instant *dashi* stock	50 ml
Canola oil	100 ml
White sesame oil	30 ml
Salt and pepper	a pinch

METHOD

· Shell prawns, leaving tail shells intact and reserving heads. Remove innards from heads and deep-fry heads for a short while

Sesame *Miso* Dressing

· Place sesame paste, *miso* paste, lemon juice, vinegar, ginger juice and *dashi* stock in a commercial blender and blitz for a few seconds until well combined. Pour canola and sesame oil in a slow, steady stream into the sesame paste with the motor running until the remaining oil is fully emulsified. Season to taste.

· Twirl the green tea soba noodles into a "nest" like heap with a fork. Arrange cooked prawn on top and garnish with *Hon Shimeji* mushrooms and prawn head. Serve with sesame miso dressing and sprinkle with chopped chives.

OOLONG TEA
Oolong Tea Steeped Quail Egg and Pork Belly
STEEPED QUAIL EGG

INGREDIENTS

Braising Liquid

Oolong tea leaves	20 g
Dark soy sauce	15 ml
Light soy sauce	100 ml
Cinnamon sticks	3
Cloves	2
Star anise	2
Chicken stock	1.5 litres
	(see Basic Techniques pg 174)
Rock sugar	25 g
Quail eggs	4
Pork belly	200 g, seasoned with five-spice powder and salt
Arrowroot starch	for thickening
Chives	4 sticks

METHOD

Braising Liquid

· Add all the braising liquid ingredients into a pot and simmer for 20 minutes. Plunge eggs into braising liquid and simmer for 10 minutes. Remove and gently crack shells but do not break.

· Return into braising liquid and steep for 1 hour. Peel shell to serve.

· Rub pork belly with five-spice powder and salt. Deep-fry then simmer in the same braising liquid for 1 hour. Once ready, remove and slice. Thicken braising liquid with arrowroot.

· Serve pork belly with tea quail egg. Drizzle with braising liquid and garnish with chives.

CRAYFISH IN
Crayfish in Tomato Jelly with Gazpacho Espuma
TOMATO JELLY

INGREDIENTS

Tomato Essence

Tomato, preferably over-ripe	800 g
Celery	400 g, roughly chopped
Basil leaves	10 g
Water	200 ml
Worcestershire sauce	a dash
Salt and sugar	to taste
Gelatine sheets	7

Crayfish tails	4, cut into 0.5-cm cubes
Crayfish claws	8
Tomato dices	20 g
Yellow frisée	a few sprigs
Tarragon	a few sprigs
Basil	a few sprigs

Gazpacho

Tomato	500 g
Red capsicum	50 g
Red onion	60 g, peeled
Cucumber	50 g
Garlic	10 g, peeled
Lemon juice	40 ml
Sugar and salt	a pinch

Garnishing

Lemon slices	
Honey tomatoes	
Black olives	
Vodka	20 ml (optional)

METHOD

Tomato Essence

· Put tomato, celery and basil leaves in a food processor and coarsely blend. Transfer the pulp into a stockpot and add water. Bring to the boil and simmer for 2 hours. Strain with muslin cloth and bring back to the boil in a stockpot. Reduce further until you get a strong tomato essence. Add Worcestershire sauce and season to taste. Pass essence through a coffee filter.

· Soften 7 gelatine sheets by immersing them in cold water. When pliable, squeeze out excess water. Add gelatine sheets to 1 litre of tomato essence.

· Pour into champagne flute and arrange cooked crayfish tails, claws, tomato dices, yellow frisée, tarragon and basil leaf. Pour and arrange in stages. Let it set a bit then continue pouring and arranging until half full.

Gazpacho

· Blend all ingredients in a food processor until smooth. Pass through a fine sieve. Season to taste with sugar and salt.

· Fill up the foammaker with gazpacho until three-quarters full. Charge up with 1 charger and shake until very frothy and light.

· Pipe foam on top of tomato jelly until up to the brim. Serve with a lemon slice, a honey tomato and an olive. If desired, serve with vodka on the espuma.

LEATHER JACKET
Leather Jacket with Saffron Sago Pearl Sauce

INGREDIENTS

Leather Jacket

Leather Jacket fillets	4, 50 g each
Salt and pepper	a pinch
Olive oil	40 ml

Saffron Sago Pearl Sauce

Water	2 litres
Sago pearls	60 g, cooked
Shallots	60 g, peeled and sliced
Thyme	1 g
Saffron	1 g
Bay leaf	1
White wine	100 ml
Fish stock	200 ml
	(see Basic Techniques pg 174)
Cream	50 ml
Cold butter	150 g, cubed
Black mustard seeds	3 g, toasted
Tomato dices	60 g
Chives	5 g, chopped

METHOD

Leather Jacket

· Season fish with salt and pepper. Heat oil and pan-fry until golden brown on both sides.

Saffron Sago Pearl Sauce

· Bring a pot of water to the boil. Boil sago pearls for 5 minutes. Turn off fire and cover pot with a lid. Let it sit until pearls turn translucent. Pass through a sieve. Refresh with icy cold water. Transfer to a bowl. Set aside.

· To make saffron beurre blanc, cook shallots, thyme, saffron, bay leaf and white wine in a pot and reduce until one-third left. Add fish stock and reduce by half. Add cream then whisk in butter cubes.

· Mix sago pearls, black mustard seeds and tomato dices in a saucepan. Add saffron beurre blanc and stir evenly.

· Serve fish with sauce. Garnish with chopped chives.

PEACH AND VODKA GRANITÉ

Peach and Vodka Granité

Peach and Vodka Granité

YIELDS 500 ML

INGREDIENTS

Fresh peach juice	400 ml
Sugar syrup	60 ml
	(see Basic Techniques pg 174)
Lime juice	40 ml
Peaches	2, cut into halves
Vodka	20 ml (optional)

Garnishing
Peach wedges

METHOD

• Mix peach juice with sugar syrup and lime juice.

• Leave in a shallow bowl in a freezer. When ice crystals start forming around the edges, scrape surface with a fork to incorporate ice. Continue freezing and scraping every 3 hours, until ice is fluffy.

• Serve a scoop of granité on top of a peach half. Add vodka on granité and garnish with peach wedges.

INGREDIENTS

Braised Veal Shank

Veal shanks	2
Salt and pepper	a pinch
Canola oil	40 ml
Mirepoix	150 g (see Glossary pg 172)
Bay leaves	2
Rosemary and thyme	3 g each
Veal stock	1.5 litres
	(see Basic Techniques pg 174)
Hoisin sauce	100 g
Tomato	40 g

Pasta Wrapper (makes about 1 kg)

Plain (all-purpose) flour	1 kg
Salt	a pinch
Egg yolks	15
Eggs	6
Olive oil	35 ml

Tortellini

Garlic	5 g, peeled and chopped
Onion	30 g, peeled and chopped
Portobello mushroom	120 g, diced
White wine	20 ml
Cream	50 ml
Veal shank	120 g, deboned and shank cut into small dices
Sage	2 g, chopped
Salt and pepper	a pinch

Sweetbread

Sweetbread	250 g, trimmed
Milk	500 ml
Water	500 ml
Salt and pepper	a pinch
Plain (all-purpose) flour	50 g
Eggs	2, for eggwash
Breadcrumbs	80 g

Garnishing

Fried capers	16
Fried sage	8
Tomato triangles	12
Potato chips	12
Toasted pine nuts	20 g
Extra virgin olive oil	

METHOD

Braised Veal Shank

- Season veal shanks with salt and pepper. Sear on high heat and set aside.

- Sauté mirepoix until lightly caramelised. Add bay leaves, rosemary and thyme.

- Add veal stock, *hoisin* sauce and tomatoes.

- Transfer veal shank to a pot. Cover with a lid and braise in oven at 160°C for 2 1/2 hours, until the meat is separated from the bone.

- Remove veal shank from pot. Cool it down and remove bones.

- Reduce braising liquid until thickened.

Pasta Wrapper

- Pour flour and salt into a food processor. Whisk in the egg yolks and eggs with a dough hook. Add olive oil and process until crumbly.

- Transfer dough onto a work table. Dust the work surface with a little flour. Knead the dough and shape into a ball.

- Wrap the dough with cling film and rest for about an hour.

Tortellini

- Sauté garlic and onion with portobello mushrooms. Deglaze with white wine. Add cream and reduce until thickened.

- Add veal shank dices. Add sage and season to taste. Cool it down.

- Divide dough into smaller portions and roll with a pasta roller into thin, even sheets.

- Using a round 7-cm cutter, cut circles from the sheet. Place 12 g of filling in the middle of each pasta wrapper.

- Fold the top half of the wrapper over the filling. Press down firmly along the edge to seal.

- Hold the sealed piece of dough between your thumb and index finger, with the sealed edge facing outwards. Fold it around your index finger and press both ends firmly together to seal and fold down the top edge.

Sweetbread

- Soak sweetbread overnight in milk.

- Drain and wash off milk. Cook in boiling water.

- Refresh with ice cold water. Trim off any excess membranes. Cut into bite-sized pieces, of about 20–30 g.

- Season with salt and pepper and dust with flour. Brush with eggwash and coat with breadcrumbs. Deep-fry until golden brown.

- Serve tortellini with a piece of sweetbread. Garnish with capers, sage, tomato triangles, potato chips and pine nuts. Drizzle with olive oil and thickened braising liquid.

Tortellini of Braised Veal Shank and Sweetbread with Veal Jus

INGREDIENTS

Beetroot	240 g, cut into small triangles and roasted
Freshly cracked black peppercorn	a pinch
Sea salt	a pinch
Olive oil	20 ml
Lemon thyme	1 g
Kikorangi blue cheese	4, 30 g each
Baby rocket	20 g
Hazelnut oil	20 ml
Hazelnut	30 g, shelled, toasted and chopped
Freshly cracked black peppercorn	a pinch

METHOD

· In a mixing bowl, toss beetroot triangles, freshly cracked black peppercorn, sea salt, olive oil and lemon thyme. Once mixed, transfer to aluminium foil.

· Fold aluminium foil into a bag and bake in an oven at 160°C for 20 minutes.

· Arrange roasted beetroot in a bowl and top with a piece of Kikorangi cheese, gratinate under a salamander or top grill until the surface is lightly melted. Arrange a few rocket leaves on top. Drizzle with hazelnut oil. Sprinkle some chopped hazelnuts and cracked black peppercorn on top. Serve warm.

ROASTED BEETROOT

Roasted Beetroot Gratinated with Triple Cream Kikorangi, Baby Rocket Salad and Toasted Hazelnut

SPICED DUCK BREAST
Spiced Duck Breast with Charred Sarawak Pineapple

INGREDIENTS

Spiced Duck Breast

Duck breast	120 g, trimmed
Five-spice powder	a pinch
Freshly cracked black peppercorn	a pinch
Salt	a pinch
Honey	1 tsp
Light soy sauce, low sodium	1 Tbsp
Canola oil	20 ml

Charred Sarawak Pineapple

Brown sugar	50 g
Sarawak pineapple	1, skinned and cut into 4 pieces, each 5 x 5 x 2-cm
Honey	30 ml
Chicken jus	100 ml
	(see Basic Techniques pg 174)
Salt and pepper	a pinch

METHOD

Spiced Duck Breast

· Season duck with five-spice powder, coarsely crushed black pepper, salt, honey and light soy sauce.

· Pan-fry duck breast, skin-side down, over medium heat, until golden brown. Turn over and roast in the oven at 150°C for 5 minutes, until just pink in the middle.

· Rest the meat for 10 minutes before slicing.

Charred Sarawak Pineapple

· Sprinkle brown sugar over pineapple. Fry on non-stick pan to slowly caramelise both sides.

· Add honey after pineapple is sealed. Reduce slightly. Reserve honey in pan. Add chicken jus and reduce. Season to taste.

· Serve charred pineapple with duck breast. Drizzle with sauce.

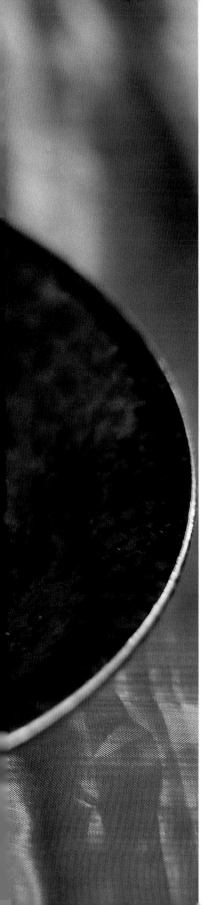

LAVENDER HONEY

Lavender Honey Ice Cream with
Aged Balsamic Vinegar Macerated Strawberry
ICE CREAM

YIELDS 4 SERVINGS

INGREDIENTS

Lavender Honey Ice Cream

Dried lavender	2 g
Milk	1 litre, warmed
Egg yolk	320 g
Cream	500 ml
Stabilizer	10 g
Trimoline	150 g
Honey	180 g

Lavender Tuiles

Soft butter	50 g
Confectioner's sugar	50 g
Egg white	50 g
Dried lavender	1 g
Plain (all-purpose) flour	50 g

Fresh strawberries	12, large, thinly sliced
Fresh strawberries	20, medium, diced
Aged balsamic vinegar	30 ml

METHOD

Lavender Honey Ice Cream

· Infuse lavender in warm milk on medium-low heat, at just below boiling point. Let it steep for 30 minutes.

· Add lavender milk to eye yolks and whisk until well-incorporated. Heat up on low heat and stir continuously until thickened.

· Cool it down. Mix in cream, stabilizer, trimoline and honey. Churn in ice cream maker according to manufacturer's instructions.

Lavender Tuiles

· Mix butter, confectioner's sugar and egg white with a whisk. When mixture is smooth, add lavender and fold in flour. Leave to rest in the refrigerator for 1 hour.

· Spread the mixture thinly on a slipat or non-stick baking sheet and bake at 180°C until golden brown. While still warm, cut the tuiles into triangles and cool on a separate tray. When cooled, keep the tuiles in an airtight container.

· Use a 7-cm pastry ring or cutter and line the sides with strawberry slices.

· Fill with 2 tablespoonfuls of macerated strawberry and top with honey lavender ice cream. Garnish with lavender tuile and a sprig of mint. Spoon over balsamic reduction. Remove ring and serve immediately.

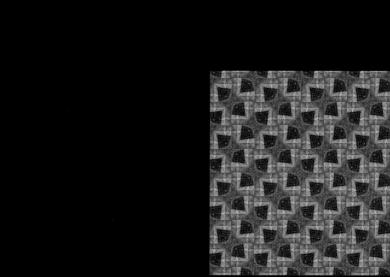

COLD CUCUMBER AND YOGHURT SOUP

Cold Cucumber and Yoghurt Soup with Fin de Claire Oyster and Royal Iranian Caviar

INGREDIENTS

Cold Cucumber and Yoghurt Soup

Cucumber	200 g, skinned and seeded
Plain yoghurt	100 ml
Oyster juice	20 ml
Lemon juice	20 ml
Dill	a few sprigs
Vegetable stock	100 ml
	(see Basic Techniques pg 174)
Salt and pepper	a pinch
Cucumber dices	80 g
Belon oysters	4, freshly shucked

Garnishing

Royal Iranian caviar	20 g
Sansho leaves	4 sprigs

METHOD

Cold Cucumber and Yoghurt Soup

- Blend cucumber, yoghurt, oyster juice, lemon juice, dill and vegetable stock together, until smooth. Season to taste.

- Serve soup with cucumber dices in the centre and shucked oyster. Garnish with caviar and *Sansho* leaves.

INGREDIENTS

Tiger prawns	12, heads removed with shells intact
Court bouillon	1 recipe
	(see Basic Techniques pg 174)

Champagne Vinegar Dressing

Citrus fruit juice (orange and lime juice)	50 ml
Champagne vinegar	50 ml
Salt and sugar	a pinch
Olive oil	250 ml

Citrus Fruit Salad

Pomelo segments	40 g, broken into bite-sized pieces
Navel orange segments	40 g
Pink grapefruit segments	80 g
Lime segments	20 g

Garnishing

Lime rind	2 g
Chervil	2 g
Freshly cracked black peppercorn	a pinch

METHOD

· Insert a bamboo skewer through the prawns and poach in court bouillon infused with lemon grass until just cooked. Remove the cooked prawns and plunge them into ice-cold water. The cold treatment yields better texture and colour to the prawns.

Champagne Vinegar Dressing

· Combine citrus fruit juice and champagne vinegar with seasoning in a mixing bowl. Pour in olive oil by the trickle and stir vigorously with a balloon whisk until the dressing is well amalgamated.

· Serve citrus fruit salad with poached prawns and drizzle with a few spoonfuls of champagne vinegar dressing. Garnish with lime rind, chervil and black peppercorn.

FRESH TIGER PRAWNS

Fresh Tiger Prawns on Citrus Fruit Salad with Champagne Vinegar Dressing

SQUID INK RISOTTO

Squid Ink Risotto with Sautéed Baby Squid and Saffron Aioli

INGREDIENTS

Risotto

Shallots	30 g, peeled and chopped
Unsalted butter	40 g
Arborio rice	100 g
Chicken stock	400 ml
	(see Basic Techniques pg 174)
Squid ink	2 g
Whipped cream	30 ml
Parmesan cheese	20 g, grated

Sautéed Baby Squid

Baby squid	120 g
Olive oil	30 ml
Garlic	5 g, peeled and chopped
Salt and pepper	a pinch
Lemon juice	10 ml

Aioli

Saffron	1 g
White wine vinegar	20 ml
Garlic	20 g, peeled and finely chopped
Egg yolks	2
Dijon mustard	1 teaspoon
Olive oil	200 ml
Parmesan cheese	12 g, shaved

METHOD

Risotto

· Sweat shallots with butter until translucent. Add Arborio rice and cook for a few more minutes, until rice is translucent.

· Add chicken stock and squid ink then simmer. Cook until al-dente, or about 12 minutes, stirring occasionally.

· Remove from heat and add whipped cream and Parmesan cheese. Season to taste.

Sautéed Baby Squid

· Sauté baby squid at high heat with olive oil and garlic until just cooked. Season to taste. Add a squeeze of lemon juice.

Aioli

· Soak saffron in white wine vinegar to bleach for 30 minutes. Remove saffron and keep aside.

· Whisk white wine vinegar with garlic, egg yolk and Dijon mustard together vigorously. Add saffron. Pour in olive oil by the trickle to incorporate. Season to taste.

· Serve risotto with sautéed baby squid on top. Garnish with a dollop of aioli and shaved Parmesan cheese.

"LAKSA" LOBSTER CAPPUCCINO
Lobster and Mango Skewer with "*Laksa*" Lobster Cappuccino

YIELDS 3 LITRES

YIELDS 3 LITRES

INGREDIENTS

Lobster

Maine lobsters	4, 500–600 g each, cut into 10 g dices
Court bouillon	1 recipe
	(see Basic Techniques pg 174)
Mango dices	4, 10 g each
Dehydrated lobster roe (optional)	

Lobster Cappuccino

Lobster heads	for making soup
Unsalted butter	200 g
Mirepoix	400 g
	(see Glossary pg 172)
Tomato paste	50 g
Tomato	200 g, roughly chopped
Laksa paste	80 g
Laksa leaves or Vietnamese mint	5 g
Brandy	100 ml
White wine	150 ml
Water	4 litres
Cream	800 ml
Cold butter	40 g

Coconut Cream

Coconut milk	100 ml
Fresh milk	100 ml
Salt	a pinch

METHOD

Lobster

- Lobsters have to be boiled in court bouillon for 10–12 minutes. Shell the lobsters. Cut lobster meat into dices. Reserve lobster heads for making cappuccino.

Lobster Cappuccino

- Crush lobster heads with a rolling pin until they are broken. Sauté heads in butter on medium heat for slow browning. Add in mirepoix and tomato paste.

- Flame it with brandy. Deglaze with white wine, add water or shellfish stock.

- Simmer for 45 minutes. Do not let it boil. Skim off the scum that floats on the surface. Add cream and reduce for further 10 minutes. Remove from heat and strain through a fine sieve.

- Return to pot and bring to the boil. Using a handheld blender, blitz with cold butter for the cappuccino effect.

Coconut Cream

- Heat up coconut milk with milk. Season lightly with salt.

- Use a handheld blender to create foam.

- Serve soup in a shot glass and top with coconut foam.

- Put a piece of lobster and a cube of mango on a skewer. Place skewer on top of the soup. Sprinkle with dehydrated lobster roe (optional).

RED MULLET "GOATFISH"

Confit of Red Mullet "Goatfish" with Warm Potato, Kalamata Olives, Tomato Salad and Tapenade Dressing

YIELDS 4 SERVINGS

INGREDIENTS

Confit of Red Mullet "Goatfish"

Goatfish fillets	4
Olive oil	250 ml
Garlic	1 bulb, lightly smashed
Thyme	1 g
Bay leaves	2
Lemon peel	4 g
Fingerling potato	2, peeled and sliced to 0.5-cm thickness
Kalamata olives	4, pitted
Oven-dried Roma tomato	2, cut into quarters
Oven-dried yellow tomato	2, cut into quarters
Caperberries	8
Basil leaves	a few sprigs, lightly brushed with olive oil

Garnishing

Sea salt	for sprinkling
Lime	1, cut into quarters
Tapenade dressing*	

Tapenade Dressing*

Garlic	5 g
Thyme	2 g
Anchovy	50 g
Capers	50 g
Black olives	150 g
Olive oil	200 ml
Lemon juice	20 ml

· Blend all the ingredients in a food processor until smooth.

METHOD

Confit of Red Mullet "Goatfish"

· Season fish. Heat olive oil with garlic, thyme, bay leaves and lemon peel, up to 65°C. Maintain heat for 20 minutes.

· Submerge goatfish inside oil for 4–6 minutes or until just cooked. Remove and drain off excess oil.

· Steam sliced potato until cooked.

· Arrange goatfish on potato slices and the rest of the ingredients. Sprinkle sea salt and serve with a lime quarter and tapenade dressing.

ROASTED CORNISH

Roasted Cornish Game Hen with Peach and Mango Salsa

GAME HEN

YIELDS 4 SERVINGS

INGREDIENTS

Roasted Cornish Game Hen

Cornish game hen breasts	4
Salt and pepper	a pinch
Thyme	1 g, chopped
Canola oil	25 ml
Clarified butter	25 g
	(see Basic Techniques pg 174)

Peach and Mango Salsa

Peach	100 g, thinly sliced
Mango	200 g, peeled and thinly sliced
Raisins	10 g, soaked in 20 ml sugar syrup for at least 2 hours
	(see Basic Techniques pg 174)
Red chilli	5 g, brunoise
Coriander leaves	2 g, chopped
Mint leaves	1 g, shredded
Lime juice	15 ml
Olive oil	60 ml
Salt and pepper	a pinch
Cherry tomatoes	4, slow-roasted
	(see Basic Techniques pg 174)

METHOD

Roasted Cornish Game Hen

· Season game hen breasts with salt, pepper and thyme. Sear in a frying pan with oil and butter until golden brown. Place game hen in a preheated oven at 160°C and roast until juices run clear and game hen is completely cooked.

Peach and Mango Salsa

· Combine all the salsa ingredients and toss gently to mix.

· Serve game hen with fruit salsa and slow-roasted cherry tomatoes.

TOMATO SORBET

Tomato Sorbet with Basil Syrup, Extra Virgin Olive Oil, Sea Salt and Freshly Cracked Black Peppercorn

YIELDS 1 LITRE

INGREDIENTS

Tomato Sorbet

Roma tomato	1 kg
Granulated sugar	150 g
Lemons	2, large, juice extracted

Basil Syrup

Basil	30 g
Flat parsley	20 g
Sugar syrup	150 ml
	(see Basic Techniques pg 174)

Garnishing

Extra virgin olive oil	
Sea salt	a pinch
Freshly cracked black peppercorn	a pinch
Basil	a few sprigs
Oven-dried tomato	

METHOD

Tomato Sorbet

- Purée tomatoes with sugar and lemon juice in a food processor and pass through a fine sieve. Taste and adjust the acidity or sweetness if necessary. Finish the sorbet in an ice cream maker and churn according to manufacturer's instructions for a smooth consistency. Freeze until firm.

Basil Syrup

- Blanch basil and parsley and refresh with ice-cold water. Drain and pat dry.

- Combine sugar syrup and blanched basil and parsley in a blender and process until leaves are finely blended. Leave syrup to steep in room temperature for at least 4 hours. Strain with a coffee strainer and discard green pulp.

- Serve tomato sorbet with basil syrup and extra virgin olive oil. Sprinkle with sea salt and black peppercorn. Garnish with a fresh sprig of basil and oven-dried tomato.

BRAISED VEAL CHEEK

Braised Veal Cheek with Wild Mushroom and Spinach Risotto

INGREDIENTS

Braised Veal Cheek

Veal cheeks	4, 80 g each
Salt and pepper	a pinch
Plain (all-purpose) flour	for dusting
Butter	40 g
Canola oil	40 ml
Mirepoix	150 g
	(see Glossary pg 172)
Thyme	2 g
Rosemary	1 g
Bay leaf	1
Garlic	4 cloves
Red wine	500 ml
Veal stock	1.2 litres
	(see Basic Techniques pg 174)
Salt and pepper	a pinch

Wild Mushroom Risotto

Onion	60 g, peeled and finely chopped
Mixed wild mushrooms	120 g
(*hon shimeiji* and morel mushrooms)	
Unsalted butter	125 g
Carnaroli rice or Arborio rice	300 g
Chicken stock	1.2 litres
	(see Basic Techniques pg 174)
Olive oil	30 ml
Onion	20 g, peeled and chopped
Thyme	1 g, chopped
Dry white wine	100 ml
Spinach leaves	100 g
Olive oil	20 ml
Garlic	5 g, finely chopped
Cream	80 ml, whipped to soft peak
Parmesan cheese	60 g, freshly grated

Garnishing

Chervil	a few sprigs
Parmesan cheese	12 g, shaved
Oven-dried tomatoes	4
Freshly cracked black peppercorn	a pinch

METHOD

Braised Veal Cheek

· Season veal cheeks with salt and pepper and dust with flour. Sear with butter and oil at medium heat until golden brown. Add a few sprigs of mirepoix, thyme, rosemary, bay leaf and garlic. Continue to cook until mirepoix turns light brown.

· Add red wine and reduce by half. Add in veal stock.

· Cover the pot and braise in the oven at 150°C for 2 hours.

· Check that the sinews have been broken down and that the veal cheeks are soft enough to be eaten with a spoon.

· Pour out half the juice and reduce until sauce coats the back of a spoon. Season. Leave veal cheek in remaining juice and set aside to cool.

Wild Mushroom Risotto

· Sweat onions with butter.

· Add in rice and sauté further until rice is evenly coated with butter and turning translucent. Add in chicken stock. Cook until al dente.

· In a separate pan, sauté both *hon shimeiji* and morel mushrooms in olive oil with chopped onions and fresh thyme. Deglaze with white wine and continue to cook until the white wine has dissipated.

· Transfer mushrooms into risotto. Stir evenly.

· Sauté spinach, with olive oil and chopped garlic, until barely wilted. Mix in risotto. Add whipped cream and Parmesan cheese before serving.

Garnishing

· Serve risotto with veal cheek sauce and topped with braised veal cheek. Garnish with a sprig of chervil, shaved Parmesan cheese, oven-dried tomato and freshly cracked black peppercorn.

INGREDIENTS

Camembert with Kataifi Pastry

Kataifi pastry	1 box
Camembert cheese portions	4, 30 g each

Red Capsicum Coulis

Red capsicum	150 g
Sugar syrup	100 ml
	(see Basic Techniques pg 174)
Lemon juice	15 ml

Garnishing

Confectioner's sugar	30 g, for dusting
Freshly cracked black peppercorn	a pinch

METHOD

Camembert with Kataifi Pastry

· Break up Kataifi pastry loosely over a rectangular area measuring 16 x 6-cm. Place a Camembert cheese portion on the pastry, near the edge of the length, and roll up to encase.

· Bake in the oven at 180°C for 4–5 minutes, until golden brown. Remove from oven.

Red Capsicum Coulis

· Burn red capsicum until charred. Put in a plastic bag and seal it. Leave for 10 minutes for it to steam in its own heat.

· Peel off skin and rinse with water. Remove seeds. Add sugar syrup and purée in a food processor to make coulis. Add lemon juice for the tangy finishing touch.

· Serve Camembert encased with Kataifi pastry on red capsicum coulis and dust with confectioner's sugar. Sprinkle black peppercorn. Serve immediately.

CAMEMBERT ENCASED
Camembert Encased with Kataifi Pastry on Charred Red Capsicum Coulis
WITH KATAIFI PASTRY

MANGO SOUP

Mango Soup with Pomelo

YIELDS 1 LITRE

INGREDIENTS

Fresh mango pulp	350 g
Granulated sugar	60 g
Lime juice	40 ml
Sparkling water	800 ml

Garnishing

Pomelo	$1/2$, broken into sacs
Mango brunoise	
Mint leaves	

METHOD

• Purée mango, sugar and lime juice in a food processor. Pass through a sieve.

• Add sparkling water to mango purée.

• Serve mango soup topped with pomelo sacs and mango brunoise. Garnish with a sprig of mint leaf. Serve well-chilled.

INGREDIENTS

Chocolate Ganache

Cream	200 ml
Trimoline	35 g
Dark chocolate	275 g, chopped
Unsalted butter	35 g, softened

Chocolate Cake

Dark chocolate	300 g, chopped
Unsalted butter	300 g, softened
Eggs	8
Egg yolks	8
Sugar	100 g
Plain (all-purpose) flour	100 g

Chocolate Tuile

Unsalted butter	50 g, softened
Confectioner's sugar	50 g
Egg white	60 g
Cocoa powder	20 g
Plain (all-purpose) flour	45 g, sieved

Orange Cardamon Ice Cream

Orange juice	500 ml
Cardamon pods	10 g
Milk	1 litre
Stabilizer	10 g
Trimoline	180 g
Cream	250 ml
Egg yolk	160 g
Granulated sugar	250 g
Orange compound	20 g

Garnishing

Orange segments	8
Blood orange segments	8
Candied orange zest	
Confectioner's sugar	for dusting

METHOD

Chocolate Ganache

· Heat up cream and trimoline to just before boiling point. Slowly pour over chopped chocolate. Stir slowly until smooth.

· Stir in butter then pour into a lined tray. Refrigerate to set for 2 hours.

Chocolate Cake

· Place chopped chocolate in a bowl and melt with bain-marie. Add in softened butter and mix well. Whisk eggs, egg yolks and sugar until churned, then fold the mixture into the chocolate mixture.

· Sieve the flour and fold it well with the chocolate mixture.

· Line cake rings with silicon paper, making sure that the paper is higher than the ring by 1-cm. Brush paper with a bit of melted butter and dust with flour. Pipe chocolate cake mixture into rings and fill up halfway.

· Cut a rectangular piece of ganache to fit into the ring. Place ganache on top of mixture. Pipe some more mixture until three-quarters full. Leave the chocolate cake in the freezer until partially frozen. Bake in an oven at 200°C for 7 minutes.

Chocolate Tuile

· Mix butter and confectioner's sugar together, followed by egg white, cocoa powder and flour. Whisk until it becomes a paste.

· Use a cardboard stencil with a 24 x 2-cm cut-out. Place on a baking tray and spread paste evenly over stencil with a palette knife.

· Roast in the oven for 5–6 minutes at 180°C. When still warm, wind tuile around the handle of a wooden spoon and leave to set. Once cooled, keep in an airtight container with a packet of food-safe silica gel.

Orange Cardamon Ice Cream

· Simmer orange juice and cardamom pods. Bring to just before boiling point, turn off fire and let cardamom infuse until essential oils are released into the juice.

· Bring milk to the boil and stir in stabilizer, trimoline and orange compound. When it has cooled down, add in cream and juice together. Chill in refrigerator then churn in ice cream maker according to manufacturer's instructions.

· Serve chocolate cake with chocolate tuile and a scoop of ice cream on top of orange and blood orange segments. Garnish ice cream with candied orange peel and dust cake with confectioner's sugar.

WARM CHOCOLATE CAKE
Warm Chocolate Cake with Orange Cardamon Ice Cream

12 - COURSE

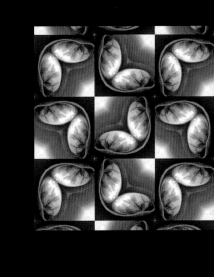

LANGOUSTINE CARPACCIO

Langoustine Carpaccio with Royal Iranian Caviar, Extra Virgin Olive Oil and Chives

YIELDS 20 SERVINGS

INGREDIENTS

Langoustine Carpaccio

Langoustine	2 kg, large, shelled
Sea salt	a pinch
Freshly cracked black peppercorn	a pinch
Poppy seeds	a pinch, toasted
Chives	1 g, chopped
Extra virgin olive oil (1% acidity)	20 ml
Extra virgin olive oil (0.5% acidity)	20 ml

Garnishing

Lime	1
Royal Iranian caviar	20 g
Chives	4 sticks
Chervil	4 sprigs

METHOD

Langoustine Carpaccio

• Prepare a rectangular terrine mould. Line mould with cling film. Lay langoustines side by side, leaving no gaps in between. The best way to do this is to lay them down, facing them in alternating directions.

• Fold in cling film and place a wooden board of appropriate size on top. Use a 1 kg weight to press down and refrigerate overnight.

• Unwrap and use a commercial meat slicer to cut into 3-mm slices. Lay a slice on a serving plate. Sprinkle sea salt, peppercorns, poppy seeds and chives. Drizzle with both types of extra virgin olive oil.

Garnishing

• Squeeze a touch of lime juice over. Garnish with a spoonful of Royal Iranian caviar and top with a chives and chervil.

SEARED TUNA AND
Seared Tuna and Salmon with Marinated Seaweed in Rice Paper Roll
SALMON

YIELDS 4 SERVINGS

INGREDIENTS

Salmon loin	80 g
Tuna loin	80 g
Shichimi Togarashi	1 tsp
Salt	to taste
Marinated seaweed (*Chuka Wakame*)	30 g
Golden *Tobiko*	5 g
Vietnamese rice paper	4 sheets

Wasabi Mayonnaise

Wasabi paste	1 tsp
Mayonnaise	50 ml

METHOD

· Season salmon and tuna loins with *Shichimi Togarashi* spice and salt. Heat oil in a non-stick frying pan and sear both salmon and tuna loins at high heat on all sides.

· Cool in the refrigerator.

· Soak rice paper in lukewarm water until soft. Remove from water and place between two pieces of absorbent cloths to dry.

· Place salmon in the centre of rice paper but closer to you. Arrange seaweed loosely next to salmon and add a few spoonfuls of *Tobiko*. Place tuna next to seaweed and away from you. Roll up tightly and chill covered with a wet cloth in the refrigerator until serving time.

Wasabi Mayonnaise

· Mix Wasabi with mayonnaise.

· Slice tuna and salmon roll just before serving and serve with a small dollop of Wasabi mayonnaise.

POACHED WHITE CLAM

Poached White Clam in Dry White Wine with Tomato Olive Salsa

YIELDS 1 KG

INGREDIENTS

Poached White Clams

White onion	30 g, peeled and diced
Dry white wine	400 ml
Leek	30 g, white part only
Bay leaves	2
White clams	1 kg, washed and scrubbed

Tomato Olive Salsa

Roma tomatoes	60 g, diced
Kalamata olives	8, julienned
Japanese pickled ginger (*gari*)	8 g, julienned
Kenya beans	60 g, blanched and diced
Extra virgin olive oil	120 ml
Verjuice	30 ml
Clam jus	80 ml
Freshly cracked black peppercorn	to taste
Sea salt	to taste

METHOD

Poached White Clams

· Sweat onions in a pot then add white wine, leek and bay leaves. Bring to the boil and add clams. Cook covered for 3–5 minutes or until most of the clams open. Reserve clam jus.

Tomato Olive Salsa

· Mix all the salsa ingredients together with 80 ml clam jus.

· Serve clam meat on salsa.

INGREDIENTS

Black Cod

Black cod fillets	4, 50 g each
Salt and pepper	a pinch

Yuzu Dressing

	200 ml
Red chilli	30 g, brunoise
Yuzu zest	1
Yuzu juice	1
Champagne vinegar	40 ml
Salt	a pinch
Canola oil	150 ml

Eringi mushroom	120 g, sliced
Olive oil	30 ml
Salt and pepper	a pinch

Garnishing

Marinated *konbu*	12 g
Broccolini	120 g, blanched

METHOD

Black Cod

· Season fish with salt and pepper. Pan-fry until golden brown on both sides. Keep the fish warm.

Yuzu Dressing

· Combine all the dressing ingredients except sunflower oil in a mixing bowl. Pour sunflower oil in by the trickle and whisk at the same time to emulsify. Season to taste. Keep aside.

· Brush *Eringi* mushrooms with olive oil and grill until cooked. Season with salt and pepper.

· Serve black cod with *Eringi* mushrooms, *konbu* and broccolini. Drizzle with *yuzu* dressing.

BLACK COD

Black Cod with *Eringi* Mushroom, Broccolini and *Yuzu* Dressing

INGREDIENTS

Pigeon Essence

Pigeon bones	600 g
Chicken bones	200 g
Dried scallops	5, large
Jin Hwa ham (Chinese air-dried ham)	20 g
Water	1 litre
Light soy sauce	1 Tbsp
Salt	a pinch

Pigeon Mousse

Chicken thigh	100 g, skinned and cut into small cubes
Pigeon	100 g, skinned and cut into small cubes
Thick cream	80 ml
Egg whites	2
Sea salt	a pinch
Ground black pepper	a pinch
Ice	3 cubes

Duck Foie Gras Tortellini

Duck foie gras	100 g
Cèpe mushroom	50 g, diced and lightly sautéed
Oregano	1 g, chopped
Pigeon mousse	200 g
Fresh pasta sheets	for making tortellini or use wanton wrappers
Eggs	2, for eggwash
Semolina flour	for dusting tray
Jasmine tea leaves	3 g per serving

METHOD

Pigeon Essence

· Trim any excess fat and remove any organs that may still be attached to the carcasses. Chop the carcasses into small pieces and rinse them thoroughly with cold water. Drain well.

· To double-boil, place pigeon and chicken bones in pocelain bowl with lid. Add dried scallops, *Jin Hwa* ham, water and light soy sauce. Steam for 3 hours. Stock should be very clear. Skim off oil particles at the top near the end of double-boiling. Season to taste.

Pigeon Mousse

· Blend all the ingredients in a food processor to a smooth paste. Pass through a sieve.

Duck Foie Gras Tortellini

· Sauté some duck foie gras at high heat for a few minutes. Fold duck foie gras, cèpe mushrooms and oregano into pigeon mousse.

· Place a spoonful of filling on pasta sheet of 8-cm diameter. Brush the edges with eggwash. Fold the top half of the pasta sheet over the filling, pressing down firmly along the edge to seal. Brush over the edges with eggwash.

· Hold the sealed piece of dough between your thumb and index finger, with the sealed edge facing outwards. Fold it around your index finger and press both ends firmly together to seal and fold down the top edge.

· Sprinkle semolina flour on tray to prevent tortellini from sticking. Place tortellini on tray.

· Plunge tortellini into boiling water and simmer until tortellini is cooked. Remove.

· Put jasmine tea leaves in infuser. Infuse in soup for 3 minutes.

· Serve essence of pigeon with tortellini.

ESSENCE OF PIGEON
Essence of Pigeon Perfumed with Jasmine Tea

STEAMED HALIBUT

Steamed Halibut with *Edamame* and Marjoram Oil

YIELDS 4 SERVINGS

INGREDIENTS

Steamed Halibut

Halibut fillets	4, 40 g each

Edamame

Edamame beans	120 g, blanched and peeled
Salt	to taste

Marjoram Oil

Fresh marjoram	30 g, blanched
Parsley	20 g, blanched
Olive oil	200 ml
Salt	to taste

Garnishing

Rocket leaves	12 g
Yellow frisée	8 g
Chervil	4 sprigs

METHOD

Steamed Halibut
- Steam halibut for 4 minutes, or until just cooked.

Edamame
- Blanch *edamame* in hot water until cooked. Plunge into ice-cold water to refresh. Remove from pods and peel off membrane. Keep beans aside.

Marjoram Oil
- Blend marjoram, parsley, olive oil and salt to a purée in a food processor. Pass through a fine sieve lined with a coffee filter.

- Before serving, plunge *edamame* into boiling salted water. Drain and mix with marjoram oil. Serve steamed halibut with marjoram oil-coated *edamame*. Garnish with rocket leaves, yellow frisée and chervil.

PAN-FRIED QUAIL

Pan-fried Quail with Spiced Duck Foie Gras and Quail Sunny-side Up

YIELDS 4 SERVINGS

INGREDIENTS

Pan-fried Quail

Boneless quails	4
Salt and coarsely cracked black peppercorn	a pinch
Rice flour	for coating quail
Canola oil	for pan-frying

Spiced Duck Foie Gras

Duck foie gras	4 slices, 40 g each
Plain (all-purpose) flour	for coating foie gras
Sea salt and freshly cracked black peppercorn	a pinch
Quail eggs	4
Mesclun salad	120 g, lightly tossed with olive oil, salt and pepper

Garnishing

Extra virgin olive oil	20 ml
Aged balsamic vinegar	20 ml

METHOD

Pan-fried Quail

· Season quail with salt and pepper. Lightly dust with rice flour. Sear at high heat, skin side down, until crispy and golden brown. Turn over and transfer to an oven. Bake at 180°C until cooked.

Spiced Duck Foie Gras

· Lightly dust foie gras with flour. At medium-high heat, pan-fry foie gras until still pink in the middle. Remove and season with sea salt and black pepper.

· Pan-fry quail eggs sunny-side up.

· Arrange foie gras then sunny-side up on top of quail. Serve with salad. Drizzle with extra virgin olive oil and balsamic vinegar.

YIELDS 1.5 LITRES

INGREDIENTS

Nashi Pear Sorbet

Nashi pear juice	800 ml
Sugar syrup	600 ml
(see Basic Techniques pg 174)	
Lemon juice	100 ml

Garnishing

Nashi pear	1, peeled and seeded

METHOD

Nashi Pear Sorbet

· Mix *Nashi* pear juice with sugar syrup and lemon juice.

· Pass through a sieve. Leave in ice cream maker to churn according to manufacturer's instructions to a sorbet texture.

· Store in the freezer for 3 hours before serving.

Garnishing

· Cut *Nashi* pear into dices and wedges. Serve sorbet on top of pear dices. Garnish with a few pear wedges.

NASHI PEAR SORBET

Nashi Pear Sorbet

ROASTED VEAL RACK

Roasted Veal Rack with Savoy Cabbage, Pancetta, Mousseline Potato and Veal Jus

INGREDIENTS

Roasted Veal Rack
Veal rack (French cut)	1, about 450 g, trimmed
Dijon mustard	1 tsp
Salt	a pinch
Thyme	1 g, chopped
Rosemary	1 g, chopped
5 peppercorns (black, white, red, green, *Szechuan*)	5 g, lightly crushed
Canola oil	50 ml

Mousseline Potato
Potato	200 g, boiled and peeled
Cream	40 ml
Unsalted butter	25 g
Salt and pepper	a pinch
Nutmeg powder	a pinch

Savoy Cabbage
Savoy cabbage	300 g, chiffonade
Unsalted butter	25 g
Shallots	30 g, peeled and sliced
Streaky bacon	20 g, cut into strips
Garlic confit	10 g
	(see Basic Techniques pg 174)
Chicken stock	40 ml
	(see Basic Techniques pg 174)
Salt and pepper	a pinch
Butter	50 g
Veal jus	150 ml
	(see Basic Techniques pg 174)

METHOD

Roasted Veal Rack
- Brush veal rack with Dijon mustard. Season with salt, thyme, rosemary, 5 peppercorns and sunflower oil. Leave to marinate for 30 minutes.

- Sear meat over medium-high heat until golden brown. Finish off in oven at 150°C for 20–25 minutes, or until medium-rare.

- Let the meat rest for 10 minutes before cutting. Portion into cutlets.

Mousseline Potato
- Incorporate cream and butter into boiled potato in a food processor. Season with salt, pepper and nutmeg powder.

- Spoon potato into a piping bag.

Savoy Cabbage
- Heat butter and sauté shallots with bacon and garlic confit until bacon is lightly browned. Add savoy cabbage then pour in chicken stock. Cook until vegetable is slightly firm or just cooked. Add a dollop of butter. Season to taste.

- Serve roasted veal cutlet with savoy cabbage and mousseline potato. Drizzle with veal jus.

Watermelon and Feta Cheese on Rosemary Skewer with Aged Balsamic Vinegar

WATERMELON AND
FETA CHEESE

YIELDS 4 SERVINGS

INGREDIENTS
Rosemary Skewers
Rosemary	8 sprigs
Yellow watermelon	8 cubes, 2-cm each
Feta cheese	8 cubes, 2-cm each
Red watermelon	8 cubes, 2-cm each

Garnishing
Extra virgin olive oil (1% acidity)	60 ml
Aged balsamic vinegar	12 ml
Lemon thyme	2 g, chopped
Rosemary	1 g, chopped

METHOD
Rosemary Skewers
• Keeping the rosemary top intact, remove the leaves from the lower parts to create a skewer.

• Using a rosemary skewer, pierce through a yellow watermelon cube, Feta cheese cube and red watermelon cube. If the rosemary skewer is very young, then pierce cubes with a bamboo skewer first before inserting rosemary skewer.

Garnishing
• Serve skewers drizzled with extra virgin olive oil and balsamic vinegar. Sprinkle with lemon thyme and rosemary.

INGREDIENTS
Panna Cotta

Vanilla bean	1
Milk	200 ml
Cream	400 ml
Gelatine sheets	4
Granulated sugar	40 g
Buttermilk	350 ml

Rhubarb Compote

Rhubarb	500 g, trimmed
Vanilla bean	1
Granulated sugar	80 g
Water	50 ml

Sauternes Jelly

Gelatine sheets	3
Sauternes wine	300 ml

METHOD
Panna cotta
- Split vanilla bean and scrape out all the seeds. Heat milk, cream and vanilla seeds gently for 10 minutes but take care not to boil.

- Soften gelatine sheets by immersing them in cold water. When pliable, squeeze out excess water. Add gelatine, sugar and buttermilk into warm cream.

Rhubarb compote
- Break rhubarb and peel off outer skin. Cut into big cubes.

- Split vanilla bean and scrape out all the seeds. Add sugar, water and vanilla seeds to rhubarb cubes and cook gently until rhubarb is broken down.

- Fill the bottom of a cocktail glass with rhubarb compote. Pour in cream until three-quarters full. Refrigerate to set.

Sauternes Jelly
- Treat gelatine sheets as before and dissolve in slightly warmed Sauternes wine. Let it cool down slightly and pour on top of panna cotta, forming a thin layer. Chill for 30 minutes. Serve.

BUTTERMILK

Buttermilk Panna Cotta with Rhubarb Compote

PANNA COTTA

VINCOTTO-
Petits Fours with Vincotto-macerated Berries
MACERATED BERRIES

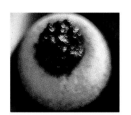

YIELDS ABOUT 20

INGREDIENTS

Petit Fours

Confectioner's sugar	130 g
Ground almonds	50 g
Plain (all-purpose) flour	50 g
Baking powder	3 g
Trimoline	10 g
Egg white	100 g, whisked until stiff
Beurre Noisette (brown butter)	80 g, warmed

Vincotto-macerated Berries

Fresh blackberries	100 g
Fresh raspberries	100 g
Vincotto	80 ml

METHOD

Petit Fours

· Combine all ingredients except egg white and brown butter in an electric mixer using the k-beater until smooth. Fold egg white carefully into mixture.

· Add brown butter in a very slow, steady stream until the mixture is thoroughly emulsified. Cover with plastic wrap and refrigerate for at least 3 hours.

· Using a piping bag, fill miniature dariole non-stick moulds two-thirds full and bake at 220°C for 5–10 minutes or until light brown depending on the size of the moulds. Cool completely before removing from moulds.

Vincotto-macerated Berries

· Soak berries in vincotto and leave in the refrigerator overnight.

· Top petits fours with vincotto-macerated berries.

BLACK AND WHITE

Black and White Sesame Tuiles

SESAME TUILES

YIELDS ABOUT 40

INGREDIENTS

Orange juice	150 g
Orange zest	from 1 orange
Castor sugar	150 g
Confectioner's sugar	150 g
Melted butter	110 g
Plain (all-purpose) flour	110 g
Ground hazelnuts	110 g
Poppy seeds	10 g
Black sesame seeds	10 g
White sesame seeds	10 g

METHOD

· Mix orange juice, zest, sugar, confectioner's sugar and melted butter with an electric mixer and whisk at low speed until smooth. Fold in flour, ground hazelnuts, poppy seeds, black and white sesame seeds. Refrigerate for at least 1 hour.

· Spread mixture thinly on silpat and bake at 200°C for 5–7 minutes until golden brown. While still warm, cut out circles with a pastry cutter and drape over a rolling pin to make tuiles.

PISTACHIO
Pistachio Friandes
FRIANDES

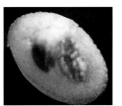

YIELDS ABOUT 70

INGREDIENTS

Butter	375 g
Castor sugar	375 g
Vanilla bean	1
Eggs	8
Ground hazelnut	500 g
Self-raising flour	175 g
Pistachio nuts	70
Walnut nuts	70

METHOD

· Combine butter and sugar until smooth.

· Add eggs and fold in ground hazelnut and flour. Split vanilla bean and scrape out the seeds. Add vanilla seeds to dough.

· Using a piping bag, fill friandes mould until three-quarters full. Top with pistachio nut and walnut, and bake at 180°C for 25 minutes.

LEMON
Lemon Tartlet
TARTLET

YIELDS 1.2 KG

INGREDIENTS

Pâté Sablée (Sandy Pastry)

Butter	360 g
Castor sugar	180 g
Egg yolks	6
Plain (all-purpose) flour	450 g, sifted
Salt	2 g
Ground almonds	90 g

Lemon Custard

Castor sugar	100 g
Corn flour	40 g
Egg yolks	4
Lemon juice	80 ml
Lemon zest	from 1 lemon
Milk	500 ml

METHOD

Pâté Sablée (Sandy Pastry)

· Mix butter, sugar and egg yolks in a food processor at high speed. Blend in flour, salt and ground almond to a paste. Chill in the refrigerator for at least 1 hour before use.

· Roll pastry out and line as many mini tartlet tins as possible, then chill in the refrigerator for at least 15 minutes. Prick the base of pastry shells with a fork and blind bake until firm at 180°C for about 10–15 minutes. Leave to cool and remove from tins.

Lemon Custard

· Combine sugar, corn flour, egg yolks, lemon juice, lemon zest and 200 ml milk in a mixing bowl. Mix well.

· In a saucepan, bring the remaining milk to just below boiling point. Add the hot milk slowly into the lemon custard mixture and stir vigorously to prevent scalding. Return the mixture into another saucepan and cook the custard at low heat or over a bain-marie, whisking continuously until the mixture thickens. Cover the surface with greaseproof paper to prevent a skin forming and let it cool.

· Spoon or pipe the cold lemon custard into the tartlets.

RASPBERRY
Raspberry Macaroons
MACAROONS

YIELDS ABOUT 40

INGREDIENTS

Egg whites	4
Castor sugar	110 g
Confectioner's sugar	110 g, sifted
Ground almonds	125 g, sifted
Red food colouring	1 drop
Raspberry jam or preserve	

METHOD

· Whisk egg whites and castor sugar with an electric mixer until firm peaks form. Gently fold in confectioner's sugar and ground almonds until just combined. Mix in red food colouring.

· Using a piping bag fitted with a plain nozzle size 8, pipe 2-cm blobs onto a baking tray lined with silicon paper, 2-cm apart. Bake at 150°C for 15 minutes or until crisp on the outside and a little soft inside. Leave to cool on trays for a few minutes before transferring to a wire rack to cool completely.

· When cooled, sandwich 2 macaroons together with a good raspberry jam.

ARBORIO RICE

Arborio rice, an Italian white rice, has short, plump grains that are high in starch content. When cooked in risottos, this soluble starch is released to give a creamy, saucelike consistency. Arborio rice is also used in rice puddings and other dishes.

BELON OYSTER

This small oyster ranges from about 4–9-cm across and is considered of superior taste. It is indigenous to France.

BEURRE NOISETTE

The french term for brown butter, it refers to butter cooked over low heat until a light hazelnut colour.

BLACK MUSTARD SEEDS

These seeds are mainly used as a pickling spice. When using black mustard seeds in cooking, add them as late as possible, so that their pungency is not completely destroyed by cooking. They are available whole, ground or powdered.

BLOOD ORANGE

A sweet-tart orange with a bright red or red-streaked white flesh, they are best eaten fresh.

BOUQUET-GARNI

The classic bouquet-garni is made up of a few bay leaves, parsley and thyme tied in cotton cloth. It is usually tied with fine string, with a length of string left attached so that the bouquet-garni can be easily retrieved. Other herbs are frequently added, such as rosemary, sage, basil, celery leaves, chervil and tarragon.

BROCCOLINI

Broccolini is a cross between broccoli and Chinese kale. It is more tender than broccoli and the stalks do not need to be peeled.

CAMEMBERT CHEESE

This cheese is made from cow's milk and has a white rind and a smooth, creamy inside. When choosing Camembert, select one that is plump and soft to the touch. Do not pick the overripe ones with hardened edges and runny and bitter inside.

CAPELIN ROE

Known as Masago in Japanese, these tiny, orange, fluorescent eggs are popularly used as topping for sushi, hand rolls and sushi rolls to enhance appearance and flavour. It is also used for spicy sushi sauce.

CARNAROLI RICE

Like Arborio rice, Carnaroli rice has short, plump grains that are high in starch content and when cooked, have a creamy, saucelike consistency so it is frequently used in risotto dishes.

CRÈME FRAÎCHE

This is a slightly matured and thickened fresh cream that has a slightly tangy, nutty flavour and a rich, velvety texture. It is used for adding to sauces and soups because it can be boiled without curdling. Crème fraîche is delicious spooned over fresh fruits or as topping or garnish for savoury or sweet dishes such as warm puddings.

CELERIAC

Celeriac is a brown coloured tuberous root that tastes like a cross between a strong celery and parsley. It is also known as celery root and celery knob and it comes from a special variety of the celery plant that has been bred specifically for its root. Peel it before eating either raw or cooked. When choosing, pick a relatively small and firm celeriac with the least rootlets and knobs. Avoid those with soft spots because those signal decay. Celeriac is best cooked in soups, stews, braises and purées.

CÈPE MUSHROOM

Also known as porcini mushroom, this wild mushroom is very popular in European cooking, especially in French and Italian cooking. This pale brown coloured mushroom has a smooth, meaty texture and a woodsy, nutty flavour. It is quite difficult to find fresh ones for sale but the dried form is readily available. Dried cèpes have to be soaked in hot water for 20–60 minutes, depending on thickness of the caps. Strain the soaking water and retain for soup, or stock for risotto. Its full flavour and velvety texture make it a special ingredient for creating elegant sauces for veal, poultry, game and pasta.

CHAMPAGNE VINEGAR

Champagne vinegar is exclusively produced in the Champagne region of France. It is a light, mild vinegar that is good for dressing delicately-flavoured salads or vegetables.

DRIED SCALLOPS

The best quality dried scallops vary from golden to light brown in colour and they are also aromatic and pleasant tasting. The bigger the scallop, the more expensive it is. Japanese scallops are generally bigger and more aromatic while Chinese dried scallops are comparatively smaller. Though they are smaller, they still retain their richness and piquant taste. Dried scallops may be used in many ways. It can be added to soup, gravy, stew, porridge, or stir-fried vegetables to enhance their flavour.

EDAMAME

Edamame are young, green, unprocessed soy beans that taste similar to baby lima beans. They are harvested just before they mature then cooked lightly and seasoned. These beans are often sold in the freezer section and should be kept frozen until ready to use. Fresh beans, purchased still in the pod, should be cooked and stored in the refrigerator.

GREEN TEA SOBA NOODLES

Also known as chasoba, green tea soba noodles are made of green tea powder, buckwheat flour and wheat flour. In a formal Japanese meal, a bowl of green tea noodles is often offered as the last course before a dessert.

KATAIFI PASTRY

Kataifi is a shredded wheat pastry from Greece. It contains no fat and has a neutral taste, so it can be used to cook both sweet and savoury dishes. It can be bought frozen.

KIKORANGI BLUE CHEESE

A blue cheese with a rich golden curd and creamy texture marbled with dense blue veining. It is mildly pungent but its flavour develops as it ages to create a smoother taste.

LAKSA LEAVES

Also known as Vietnamese mint, the leaves of this wild herb have a strong fragrance and are used for a special spicy noodle dish in Singapore called Laksa. The leaves go particularly well with dishes with sweet and sour sauces.

MIREPOIX

A mixture of diced carrots, onions, celery and herbs sautéed in butter. It is used for seasoning sauces, soups and stews. It can also be used as a bed on which to braise foods, usually meats or fish.

PALM SUGAR (*GULA MELAKA*)

Also known as jaggery and coconut sugar, palm sugar is produce by boiling down the sap of various varieties of palm tree. It has a coarse and sticky texture and is brown in colour.

SAUTERNES WINE

A sweet dessert wine from the Sauternes region of western France made from Sauvignon Blanc or Semillon grapes. "Sauterne" without the ending "s" usually refers to an inexpensive semisweet Californian wine.

SILPAT

The silpat is a flat, non-stick baking mat made of silicon for baking cookies and patisseries.

SAGO PEARLS

Pearl-shaped balls processed from starch extracted from sago palms. It is similar to tapioca.

VERJUICE

An acidic, sour liquid produced from unripe fruit, primarily grapes. Used in preparation of sauces and mustards to heighten flavour, it is available in gourmet food stores.

YUZU

A sour Japanese citrus fruit which is about the size of a tangerine. Yuzu is used almost exclusively for its aromatic rind, which has an aroma that is distinct from lemons and limes or any other Western citrus fruit. Yuzu rind is used for garnishing or small slivers of it are added to various dishes to enhance their flavour.

BEEF STOCK
Yields 3 litres
Ingredients
Beef bones	2 kg
Onion	200 g, peeled and diced
Celery	150 g, diced
Leek	150 g, diced
Carrot	100 g, peeled and diced
Bay leaf	1
Water	4 litres

Method
Trim any excess fat from the bones. Rinse them thoroughly with cold water. Drain well.

Place bones into a stockpot and cover with water. Slowly simmer while carefully skimming any impurities and fat that floats on the top of the pot. After most of the fat or froth has been removed, add onion, celery, leek, carrot and bay leaf and simmer for 1 hour 30 minutes.

Let the stock rest for at least 15 minutes before straining with a fine-mesh strainer. Discard the remaining cloudy stock at the bottom of the pot.

CHICKEN STOCK
Yields 3 litres
Ingredients
Chicken carcasses	2 kg
Onion	200 g, peeled and diced
Celery	150 g, diced
Leek	150 g, diced
Carrot	100 g, peeled and diced
Bay leaf	1
Water	4 litres

Method
Trim any excess fat and remove any organs that may still be attached to the carcasses. Chop the carcasses into small pieces and rinse them thoroughly with cold water. Drain well.

Place the chopped carcasses into a stockpot and cover with water. Slowly simmer while carefully skimming any impurities and fat that floats on the top of the pot. After most of the fat or froth has been removed, add onion, celery, leek, carrot and bay leaf and simmer for 1 hour 30 minutes.

Let the stock rest for at least 15 minutes before straining with a fine-mesh strainer. Discard the remaining cloudy stock at the bottom of the pot.

CHICKEN JUS
Ingredients
Chicken bones	1.5 kg, chopped
Onion	150 g, peeled and diced
Carrot	150 g, peeled and diced
Celery	100 g, diced
Garlic	3 cloves
Tomato paste	1 tablespoon
Bay leaf	1
Black peppercorn	5 g
Water	6 litres

Method
Roast the chicken bones in a preheated oven at 200°C in a roasting pan, turning the bones occasionally until evenly brown. Add the vegetables into the roasting pan and roast until golden brown.

Remove the roasting pan from the oven and transfer the bones into a stockpot. Drain all excess fat from the roasting pan and place the pan on top of a stove over high heat. Deglaze the pan with at least 1 litre of water and bring to the boil, scraping the bottom with a wooden spoon to loosen the caramelised sugars.

Pour the deglazing liquid into the stockpot and add the remaining water. Slowly bring the stock to a simmer and skim off fat and impurities that float on the surface. Simmer the stock for at least 3-4 hours and pass through a fine-mesh sieve. Strain the stock for the second time through a cheesecloth. Make a reduction of the veal stock until a thin sauce-like consistency is attained.

CLARIFIED BUTTER
Heat up butter to separate fat and milk solids. The milk solids will sink to the bottom. Scoop up the top layer to use. It does not burn easily like normal butter.

COURT BOUILLON
Yields 2.5 litres
Ingredients
Carrot	50 g, sliced
White onion	50 g, sliced
Leek	40 g, white part only, sliced
Celery	40 g, sliced
Bay leaves	2
White peppercorn	5 g
Thyme	1 g
Sea salt	25 g
Water	2 litres
White wine vinegar	30 ml
White wine	750 ml

Method
Place all vegetables, herbs and seasoning in a muslin cloth and tie together. Bring water, wine and vinegar to the boil and add muslin cloth bundle. Simmer for 15–20 minutes then steep for 30 minutes. Bring court bouillon back to the boil.

DUCK JUS
Ingredients
Duck bones	1.5 kg, chopped
Onion	150 g, peeled and diced
Carrot	150 g, peeled and diced
Celery	100 g, diced
Garlic	3 cloves
Tomato paste	1 tablespoon
Bay leaf	1
Black peppercorn	5 g
Water	6 litres

Method
Roast the duck bones in a preheated oven at 200°C in a roasting pan, turning the bones occasionally until evenly brown. Add the vegetables into the roasting pan and roast until golden brown.

Remove the roasting pan from the oven and transfer the bones into a stockpot. Drain all excess fat from the roasting pan and place the pan on top of a stove over high heat. Deglaze the pan with at least 1 litre of water and bring to the boil, scraping the bottom with a wooden spoon to loosen the caramelised sugars.

Pour the deglazing liquid into the stockpot and add the remaining water. Slowly bring the stock to a simmer and skim off fat and impurities that float on the surface. Simmer the stock for at least 3-4 hours and pass through a fine-mesh sieve. Strain the stock for the second time through a cheese-cloth. Make a reduction of the veal stock until a thin sauce-like consistency is attained.

FISH STOCK
Yields 3 litres
Ingredients

Fish bones	2 kg
Onion	200 g, peeled and diced
Celery	150 g, diced
Leek	150 g, diced
Fennel	100 g, sliced
Bay leaf	1
Water	3.5 litres

Method
Chop the fish bones with a cleaver and rinse them with cold running water, until the water runs clear. Make sure to remove any visible bloodlines and veins from the fish bones.

Place the bones into a stockpot and cover with water. Gently bring the stock to a simmer, remove any impurity and fat that floats to the top. Add onion, celery, leek, fennel and bay leaf. Continue simmering the stock gently for 30 minutes, skimming off any remaining fat and scum.

Let the stock rest for at least 15 minutes. This will allow any particles to settle at the bottom of the stockpot. Strain the stock gently through a fine-mesh strainer using a ladle instead of pouring directly through; this will prevent clouding of the stock. Discard any remaining cloudy stock found at the bottom of the pot.

GARLIC CONFIT
Wrap garlic with thyme, olive oil, salt and pepper in aluminium foil. Cook in the oven at slow heat at 150°C until very soft.

LAMB JUS
Ingredients

Lamb bones	1.5 kg, chopped
Onion	150 g, peeled and diced
Carrot	150 g, peeled and diced
Celery	100 g, diced
Garlic	3 cloves
Tomato paste	1 tablespoon
Bay leaf	1
Black peppercorn	5 g
Water	6 litres

Method
Roast the lamb bones in a preheated oven at 200°C in a roasting pan, turning the bones occasionally until evenly brown. Add the vegetables into the roasting pan and roast until golden brown.

Remove the roasting pan from the oven and transfer the bones into a stockpot. Drain all excess fat from the roasting pan and place the pan on top of a stove over high heat. Deglaze the pan with at least 1 litre of water and bring to the boil, scraping the bottom with a wooden spoon to loosen the caramelised sugars.

Pour the deglazing liquid into the stockpot and add the remaining water. Slowly bring the stock to a simmer and skim off fat and impurities that float on the surface. Simmer the stock for at least 3-4 hours and pass through a fine-mesh sieve. Strain the stock for the second time through a cheesecloth. Make a reduction of the veal stock until a thin sauce-like consistency is attained.

SLOW-ROASTED CHERRY TOMATOES
Season tomatoes with salt, pepper, sliced garlic, basil, balsamic vinegar and olive oil. Slow-roast in the oven at 70°C for 30–45 minutes.

SUGAR SYRUP
For 100 ml sugar syrup, use 50 ml water and 50 g castor sugar. To make other amounts of syrup, always use equal parts of water and sugar. Heat up and stir until all the sugar is dissolved.

PORT WINE AND BALSAMIC VINEGAR REDUCTION
Ingredients

Port wine	200 ml
Balsamic vinegar	200 ml

Method
Simmer port wine and balsamic vinegar over low heat and reduce until syrupy.

VEAL JUS
Ingredients

Veal knuckle bones	1.5 kg, chopped
Onion	150 g, peeled and diced
Carrot	150 g, peeled and diced
Celery	100 g, diced
Garlic	3 cloves
Tomato paste	1 tablespoon
Bay leaf	1
Black peppercorn	5 g
Water	6 litres

Method
Roast the veal bones in a preheated oven at 200°C in a roasting pan, turning the bones occasionally until evenly brown. Add the vegetables into the roasting pan and roast until golden brown.

Remove the roasting pan from the oven and transfer the bones into a stockpot. Drain all excess fat from the roasting pan and place the pan on top of a stove over high heat. Deglaze the pan with at least 1 litre of water and bring to the boil, scraping the bottom with a wooden spoon to loosen the caramelised sugars.

Pour the deglazing liquid into the stockpot and add the remaining water. Slowly bring the stock to a simmer and skim off fat and impurities that float on the surface. Simmer the stock for at least 3-4 hours and pass through a fine-mesh sieve. Strain the stock for the second time through a cheesecloth. Make a reduction of the veal stock until a thin sauce-like consistency is attained.

VEAL STOCK
Ingredients

Veal knuckle bones	1.5 kg, chopped
Onion	150 g, peeled and diced
Carrot	150 g, peeled and diced
Celery	100 g, diced
Garlic	3 cloves
Bay leaf	1
Black peppercorn	5 g
Water	10 litres

Method
Roast the veal bones in a preheated oven at 200°C in a roasting pan, turning the bones occasionally until evenly brown. Add the vegetables into the roasting pan and roast until golden brown.

Remove the roasting pan from the oven and transfer the bones into a stockpot. Drain all excess fat from the roasting pan and place the pan on top of a stove over high heat. Deglaze the pan with at least 1 litre of water and bring to the boil, scraping the bottom with a wooden spoon to loosen the caramelised sugars.

Pour the deglazing liquid into the stockpot and add the remaining water. Slowly bring the stock to a simmer and skim off fat and impurities that float on the surface. Simmer the stock for at least 3-4 hours and pass through a fine-mesh sieve. Strain the stock for the second time through a cheesecloth. Make a reduction of the veal stock until a thin sauce-like consistency is attained.

VEGETABLE STOCK
Yields 3 litres
Ingredients

Carrot	200 g
Leek	400 g
Onion	400 g
Fennel bulb	100 g
Bay leaf	2
Thyme	2 g
Fennel seeds	1 g
Orange zest	3 g
Lemon zest	3 g
Parsley stems	20 g
Water	4 litres

Method
Place all ingredients into a stockpot and cover with water. Bring to a simmer, skimming impurities, and cook for 40 minutes.

Let the stock steep for 1 hour before straining through a fine-mesh strainer.

Standard spoon and cup measurements used are: 1 tsp = 5 ml, 1 dsp = 10 ml, 1 Tbsp = 15 ml, 1 cup = 250 ml. *All measures are level unless otherwise stated.*

LIQUID AND VOLUME MEASURES

Metric	Imperial	American
5 ml	$^1/_6$ fl oz	1 tsp
10 ml	$^1/_3$ fl oz	1 dsp
15 ml	$^1/_2$ fl oz	1 Tbsp
60 ml	2 fl oz	$^1/_4$ cup (4 Tbsp)
85 ml	$2^1/_2$ fl oz	$^1/_3$ cup
90 ml	3 fl oz	$^3/_8$ cup (6 Tbsp)
125 ml	4 fl oz	$^1/_2$ cup
180 ml	6 fl oz	$^3/_4$ cup
250 ml	8 fl oz	1 cup
300 ml	10 fl oz ($^1/_2$ pint)	$1^1/_4$ cups
375 ml	12 fl oz	$1^1/_2$ cups
435 ml	14 fl oz	$1^3/_4$ cups
500 ml	16 fl oz	2 cups
625 ml	20 fl oz (1 pint)	$2^1/_2$ cups
750 ml	24 fl oz ($1^1/_5$ pints)	3 cups
1 litre	32 fl oz ($1^3/_5$ pints)	4 cups
1.25 litres	40 fl oz (2 pints)	5 cups
1.5 litres	48 fl oz ($2^2/_5$ pints)	6 cups
2.5 litres	80 fl oz (4 pints)	10 cups

DRY MEASURES

Metric	Imperial
30 g	1 ounce
45 g	$1^1/_2$ ounces
55 g	2 ounces
70 g	$2^1/_2$ ounces
85 g	3 ounces
100 g	$3^1/_2$ ounces
110 g	4 ounces
125 g	$4^1/_2$ ounces
140 g	5 ounces
280 g	10 ounces
450 g	16 ounces (1 pound)
500 g	1 pound, $1^1/_2$ ounces
700 g	$1^1/_2$ pounds
800 g	$1^3/_4$ pounds
1 kg	2 pounds, 3 ounces
1.5 kg	3 pounds, $4^1/_2$ ounces
2 kg	4 pounds, 6 ounces

OVEN TEMPERATURE

	°C	°F	Gas Regulo
Very slow	120	250	1
Slow	150	300	2
Moderately slow	160	325	3
Moderate	180	350	4
Moderately hot	190/200	370/400	5/6
Hot	210/220	410/440	6/7
Very hot	230	450	8
Super hot	250/290	475/550	9/10

LENGTH

Metric	Imperial
0.5 cm	$^1/_4$ inch
1 cm	$^1/_2$ inch
1.5 cm	$^3/_4$ inch
2.5 cm	1 inch

ABBREVIATION

tsp	teaspoon
Tbsp	tablespoon
g	gram
kg	kilogram
ml	millilitre